Finding Glory in the Thorns

Hope & Purpose in Life's Painful Seasons

Finding GLORY in the thorns

Hope & Purpose in Life's Painful Seasons

Larry & Lisa Jamieson

AMBASSADOR INTERNATIONAL
GREENVILLE, SOUTH CAROLINA & BELFAST, NORTHERN IRELAND

www.emeraldhouse.com

Finding Glory in the Thorns

Hope & Purpose in Life's Painful Seasons

www.walkrightin.org

Printed in the United States of America

ISBN 978-1-932307-87-0

Cover design & Page Layout by David Siglin of A&E Media
Author photo: www.erinjohnsonphoto.com

Scripture taken from the HOLY BIBLE, NEW INTERNATIONAL VERSION®. Copyright © 1973, 1978, 1984 International Bible Society. Used by permission of Zondervan. All rights reserved.

The "NIV" and "New International Version" trademarks are registered in the United States Patent and Trademark Office by International Bible Society. Use of either trademark requires the permission of International Bible Society.

AMBASSADOR INTERNATIONAL
Emerald House
427 Wade Hampton Blvd.
Greenville, SC 29609, USA
www.emeraldhouse.com

AMBASSADOR PUBLICATIONS
Providence House
Ardenlee Street
Belfast, BT6 8QJ
Northern Ireland, UK
www.ambassador-productions.com

The colophon is a trademark of Ambassador

This book is published in association with
Patti M. Hummel, President & Agent
The Benchmark Group LLC, Nashville, TN
benchmarkgroup1@aol.com

DEDICATED TO ALEX AND ERIN
*who courageously, patiently, humbly, and enthusiastically
sing with us the Song of Life*

Contents

PART 1

Our Journey

PART 2

The Way to Glory

Acknowledgements

Finding Glory in the Thorns is a product of tremendous partnership. We thank Almighty God who keeps giving us tangible pictures of His holiness. We visibly see, over and over again, that You are powerfully and lovingly present through it all.

Special thanks to those of you who have allowed us to share your stories so that others may see the eternal Kingdom perspective… Alex and Erin, Judd, Mary Ann and family, Perry and Di, Bruce and Barb (with Nathan), Marcia and Amanda, Lois, Neal and Vickie (with Raheem, Destiny, Sarah, and Josiah).

Every team is spurred on by its cheerleaders…Grammie and Grampy, your networking, encouragement, and experience keep us believing in dreams. Mom and Dad, your vision for the potential in Carly, in her story and within us keeps stirring our courage and hope. Lori, Darren, Nathan, and Danielle, you always prayed and never doubted.

We extend love and gratitude to…Kirk and Kari and all your little "retreat staffers," your sense of humor, creativity, generosity, hospitality gifts, gracious reading, and loyal friendship breathe fresh air into us on a regular basis. Our caregiver team, you demonstrate relentless love and energy towards Carly and her education so that our family can fully live and widely share.

We have a most treasured gift in knowing that at almost any moment, we are lifted by someone in prayer. Our hearts weep and dance for the partnership of our "Carly Update" team. You stood with us even before we knew what raging waters were ahead. You have prayed us through each season of heavy flooding and shouted for joy with us every time there was a faith-crossing to be made on dry ground. We are forever grateful to you.

May the harvest season be plentiful — to God be all glory!

Introduction

Many wonder how the parents and families of children with severe developmental challenges ever survive, many more marvel at those who learn to thrive. For many parents the challenges presented by a child with severe health and developmental issues are more than they can endure. Many marriages fail, many lose their faith and many tragically never recover. But, a precious few learn some invaluable lessons about life and faith that can often only be learned through such pain and helplessness. They not only survive, but flourish.

In *Finding Glory in the Thorns*, Larry and Lisa Jamieson recount their incredible trials in attempting to help their third daughter survive debilitating health and developmental issues. As they relate their journey from agony and desperation to understanding and acceptance, they provide an inspiring lesson for all of us who are seeking to understand life's lessons and our relationship to God.

This is not just a book for the parents of hurting and challenged children although it provides invaluable lessons for those parents. Rather, it is a book that provides invaluable lessons for everyone who struggles when they hit bumps in the road or, as in the Jamieson's case, the road disappears into a sink hole so enormous that they cannot believe they will ever crawl out of it let alone ever find their way home. They found their way and will help many others who share their story and understand their message find their way home as well.

Finding Glory in the Thorns is honest, insightful and a valuable tool for everyone attempting to understand what it really means to surrender to God's will.

ROBERT J. DOMAN JR., FOUNDER AND DIRECTOR
National Association for Child Development
www.nacd.org

Prologue

There are days when we wonder why it is necessary or even appropriate for us to tell this story. After all, our story is not as remarkable as it sometimes may seem. Thousands of families parent children with special needs or face life-altering medical issues every day. Legitimately painful seasons in life take many forms. So why have we sensed this leading from the earliest days to share our story? Why has God continued to impress upon us the need to set aside our fears, our frequent cravings for more privacy, our concerns about being judged or misunderstood, and our overwhelming sense of vulnerability?

It's not enough to say that God wants us to tell our story because he's uniquely gifted us to be particularly articulate, creative, or entertaining storytellers. It's not fair or true to suggest we have some superior wisdom (after all, any wisdom we do have has always come from God's Word or through His people to us). No, the single greatest reason why we believe God has called us to share this story is because He said so. It's simply an act of obedience. We have grown to appreciate the truth that God's power to transform lives is released when we live transparently with each other. It is in the ripples of our intersecting lives that God's power is released to do a mighty work for His glory. That is true for us and it is true for you. It is in the domino effect of shared or resonating experiences, especially experiences involving hardship and suffering, that we are most significantly changed and God's glory is best revealed.

We have also written this book because the Bible tells us that our challenges can be an encouragement. God promises that the comfort given to our family by the Holy Spirit can be your comfort too, that our troubles can be for your benefit and your salvation. What amazing economy. What an amazing reason to maintain hope in adversity. What amazing grace!

Praise be to the God and Father of our Lord Jesus Christ, the Father of compassion and the God of all comfort, who comforts us in all our troubles, so that we can comfort those in any trouble with the comfort we ourselves have received from God. For just as the sufferings of Christ flow over into our lives, so also through Christ our comfort overflows.
2 CORINTHIANS 1:3-5

For purposes of organization, Part 1 of this book recounts the high points and low points of our journey. Part 2 explores the most pressing questions each of us has asked along the way:

How do I SURRENDER to God's solutions and timing?

How do I keep the kind of FAITH it will take to make it through this?

How do I hold on to HOPE when the risk of disappointment seems so real?

How do I experience JOY when this challenge is so consuming?

Is it worth SHARING my life with others, ugly parts and all, when asking for help and giving it are so hard?

We believe these five core questions reflect the longings of a suffering soul and are rather universal in the experience of a person or family walking through any significant challenge, particularly one involving a life-altering disability or a threatening medical condition. We consider it one of God's most amazing gifts that He has walked us through a process of discovering fundamental answers to these questions. This book is designed to help us all resonate and grow together through the life-lifting discoveries our Lord wants to share with us.

While we know God can use a book like this to help you grow in your life and your relationship with Jesus, we believe that God works even more powerfully to magnify His beautiful, transforming work in the context of a Christ-centered small group, community. With that in mind, we prayerfully challenge you to seek out such an opportunity.

The various small groups we have been a part of (both individually and as a couple or family) have often been a "lifeline" for us. Small groups have been significantly instrumental in helping us experience true fullness of life as we believe God intended. Those groups have given us support on practical and spiritual levels beyond compare. There are many kinds of small groups — women's groups, men's groups, couple's groups, family groups, support groups, and so on. The most important thing is not what kind of group it is but whether the group is drawing individuals toward Christ Himself. The primary activities of the group should be prayer, reflecting on God's word, and Christ-centered fellowship. (That is, in fact, how scripture models fruitful Christian community in Acts 2.) Fellowship alone will not be as satisfying or eternally beneficial.

If you have never been in a small group Bible Study, we pray that you will be inspired to find one and get started immediately. If you have been in a small group but are not now, or the group you are in is distracted from a focus on Christ, we urge you to find a group that is truly Christ-centered and don't turn back. If you are currently in a small group experience that provides regular opportunities for prayer, the Word of God, and fellowship then praise the Lord!

Let us not give up meeting together, as some are in the habit of doing, but let us encourage one another—and all the more as we see the Day approaching.
HEBREWS 10:25

We are so excited about what God is doing! We pray with love and gratitude for the journeys we share together.

PART I
Our Journey

Our Season of Lost Dreams

I cry aloud to God, and he will hear me.

In the day of my trouble I seek the Lord;

In the night my hand is stretched out without wearying;

My soul refuses to be comforted.

When I remember God, I moan;

When I meditate, my spirit faints.

You hold my eyelids open;

I am so troubled that I cannot speak.

PSALM 77:1-4

Chapter 1:
Surviving the Island

The afternoon sun that late July day tried its best to penetrate the tree canopy overhead. The heat and humidity combined with our brisk pace to make for a sweaty trek across Stockton Island. Our uncertainty and anxiety over a garbled voice message on Lisa's cell phone drove us on our quest for a consistent signal. My hope was that the far southern tip of the island would bring clearer access to the mainland. But I knew that there was no guarantee.

It was the summer of 2003 and we were enjoying our seventh annual sailing excursion in and around the Apostle Islands of Lake Superior. Our good friends Ron and Nancy hosted us aboard their thirty-four foot Catalina sailboat, Second Gift. Every year, we looked forward with great anticipation to our adventures in the islands. The weather and wind were always an unknown, but the fellowship, food, and time to relax and recharge away from the realities of our regular lives never disappointed.

After a great day of plying the waters of Lake Superior, we had reached that point in the afternoon where we needed to determine a safe anchorage for the night. We tuned in to the maritime forecast to see what the wind direction would be for the night and reviewed the island maps for suitable options. Our conclusion was that Julian Bay on Stockton Island's southeast shore should provide us with a protected place to comfortably anchor. We brought in the sails and motored off toward our destination.

On our way down the eastern side of Stockton Island, Lisa realized that she had a cell phone message. Her mind immediately raced to our three daughters back in the suburbs of Minneapolis. Alex was ten years old and Erin was eight. Carly, five years old, had been diagnosed with Angelman Syndrome, a genetic condition severely affecting all areas of her development. The girls were in the care of our loved and trusted friend Katie. Since Katie had accepted the call to become our primary caregiver support for Carly, she had accumulated much experience responding to seizures and other issues that could arise due to Carly's condition. She knew well our need to get uninterrupted time away so any phone call from home could to be an emergency in nature.

Cell coverage in the islands was spotty at best. As Lisa attempted to retrieve the message, what she heard was Katie's mostly unintelligible voice. The only words that could be clearly made out were "Carly" and "seizure." Since Carly had experienced several grand mal episodes, Lisa's thoughts immediately focused on the need to make contact quickly. With panic in her eyes, she called me to the bow of the boat to tell me of the message. We stood there pondering the possibilities as we were suddenly swept back into the realities of life with Carly. Her first five years of life had been filled with challenges and trials and stresses that no person or family should have to face. Our mental state as parents had often teetered on the precipice of doubt and despair, which made a rare weekend away much sweeter and more important. But none of that mattered now.

We had to decide what to do. One option was to abort our plan to anchor in Julian Bay and make the two-to-three hour voyage back to the marina instead. Once on land, we would have access to a reliable phone and be able to leave at once, if necessary, for the five-hour drive home. But if we were misinterpreting the message, we would be forced to stay in the marina overnight and lose our last night of the gentle rocking and quiet solitude of an Apostle Island bay anchorage. I weighed our intense need to be away against the possibilities of a medical emergency at home. My parenting instincts waged war with my self-centered thoughts of personal preservation. I decided on an alternative course of action.

We would continue on to Julian Bay to anchor the boat. Once there, Lisa and I would swim to shore and then hike to the far southern point of Stockton Island where we would have the best chance of establishing a cell phone connection with the mainland. With the boat securely anchored, Lisa jumped into the frigid waters of Lake Superior to begin her swim. Due to the depth of the keel, it was necessary to anchor quite some distance from shore. I am not a great swimmer, so I normally take a flotation cushion along with me to use under my chest. But we weren't sure how to keep the cell phone dry during the swim, so Ron volunteered to paddle me in to shore in Second Gift's dinghy. Once we were on the shore, Lisa and I began our hike. Ron was to stay with the dinghy at the shore prepared to ferry us back out to the sailboat.

That Saturday had been one of those picture perfect days for sailing on Lake Superior—eighty degrees with a steady wind and not a cloud in the sky. But as we began to walk along the trail that led to the south end of the island, I quickly noticed that the thick tree coverage took away the Lake Superior-cooled breezes that made it quite comfortable on the boat. Instead, it was humid and sticky on the island. I began to imagine that I was somewhere in a rain forest jungle rather than on an island in the largest fresh water lake in the world, a lake that has an average summertime surface temperature of fifty-four degrees! Dressed only in a swimsuit, the sweat quickly began to drip off me, and the black flies made their presence very apparent. Lisa and I found ourselves swatting each other's backs as we walked even more briskly to shorten their feast.

In those infrequent times when we broke out of the trees into a clearing, we began to notice clouds gathering overhead. Initially, they were fluffy white, beautiful clouds, but they didn't stay that way for long. Our view to the west was completely obscured by the trees so we had no idea what weather was to come. The trail we were on was fairly well maintained alternating between hard-packed dirt and small logs placed end-to-end. But, in some places, the hard-packed dirt was replaced by a couple of inches of thick mud. I began to wonder what else might be in the mud as I imagined all of the deer that must be on the island. I have also since learned that Stockton Island has one of the most concentrated populations of black bears in the world. I'm glad Lisa didn't know that before we left the beach!

The composition of the mud was perhaps more important to me than to the average person. You see, I have lymphedema in my right leg below the knee. This means that the lymphatic fluid my body produces tends to pool in my lower right leg, providing a warm, protein-rich environment for infections to rage! I also have eczema on the bottom of that foot, which means that I often have the perfect entry points for bacteria and fungi. What I was walking through with bare feet as we headed south could have a big impact on my health. Lisa tried to make jokes about the mud but I could tell she was concerned. I didn't have time to worry. We still had no cell phone coverage!

We knew there were campsites and a ranger station at the south end of the island, and Lisa let me know that she was hopeful we would find a bathroom there. Just about then we heard the first rumble of far-off thunder. This wasn't quite working out as I had planned. I knew Ron would not be pleased, as he was always extra cautious about the weather when sailing.

It seemed to take a long time to get to our destination. It was probably only a matter of fifteen or twenty minutes, but it seemed much longer. When we arrived, we found the ranger station closed. The sun that had been so strong all day was now completely masked by a thickening layer of clouds. The thunder, still off in the distance, became more frequent. We walked to the far south point of the island. I pulled the cell phone out of my pocket and saw what I had seen every other time I had checked during our journey—no signal at all. Our trip had been for naught. The emotions that flooded through me were a high-intensity mix of frustration, anger, humor, and panic. I looked up at the sky and saw that the storm was quickly approaching.

Trees, water, and lightning are a deadly mixture. At that moment, the folly of my decision hit me like a slap in the face.

We had come a long way for nothing, only to face a daunting, dangerous return trip to the relative safety of Second Gift. There would be no walking on the way back.

Trying to mask the deep concern I felt inside, I told Lisa we were going to have to jog. Neither of us was in particularly good shape, and the air was still warm and growing even more humid. I no longer made occasional checks for a cell phone signal. There was no time. The thunder was getting close.

At one point in the middle of a densely wooded are along the path, Lisa told me she could go no farther without a bathroom break. "You've got to be kidding me!" I blurted as I looked through the treetops at darkening clouds.

"I HAVE TO GO," my wife growled. In an instant, Lisa's facial expression replaced death-by-lightning at the top of my immediate list of fears. Seeing no signs of either passersby or portable facilities, she dismissed any risk. Right there in her swimsuit, she squatted on the side of that path holding my arm and took care of her business.

Not more than a minute later, we met a park ranger hurriedly heading in the opposite direction.

I asked the ranger how far it was to the beach at Julian Bay and he replied that it was just up ahead a few minutes. He also confirmed that there was no telephone land line available.

We continued running—the sweat now pouring off of me, the thunder crackling overhead, and the first drops of rain falling from the sky. We were both exhausted but I could see in the distance an opening where the trail met the beach at Julian Bay. Maybe we were going to make it after all!

When we came up over the rise where the land meets the beach, we found a sight that we were both completely unprepared for—no Ron, and no dinghy! I looked out at the Second Gift and saw the dinghy tied up to her stern. Ron, not knowing what had become of us and understandably fearful of the bad weather, had rowed back out to his sailboat without us and was hunkered down with his wife in the cabin. Lisa walked right out into the water to begin the swim back to the boat. She turned around to see me, dumbfounded, standing on the shore.

"How had we come to this?" I asked myself. I was facing a swim of a distance I wouldn't normally even think about trying without a flotation device of some kind. And I was already completely spent from running about two miles from the south end of the island. But staying on the shore was not an option since the lightning overhead was becoming more frequent. There was no shelter to be found. I decided I would have to swim for it.

I still had our cell phone in my pocket and I knew I had to do something with that. After scanning the shoreline, I found a long-overturned tree whose roots might provide some protection from the rain. So I hid the phone as far under the roots as I could and scrambled out into the water.

The cold water took my breath away as I dove in. I swam for a while and then rolled over onto my back to float while catching my breath. I hadn't gone far when I looked up to see Ron untying the dinghy and climbing in to come for me. The lightning flashed and the thunder crashed all around. The rain poured down. I was terrified. When Ron finally got to me, I was almost too exhausted to climb into the dinghy. He managed to help me in without capsizing, and he frantically rowed back out to the sailboat. Lisa was already aboard and, as I struggled to catch my breath, the three of us scrambled down into the cabin.

The journey was over, but we still didn't know anything more than when we had left. All the hiking, running, swimming, and praying had not resulted in any tangible progress.

It Wasn't Supposed to Be This Way

A couple of days later, I lay in a hospital bed running a high fever and being pumped with antibiotics for a potentially life-threatening cellulitis infection in my leg. The message from home turned out to be a concern related to Carly's seizure medications. It was not an emergency after all but an imminent issue that needed attention.

Lisa and I took stock. The whole situation left us realizing how critical it was going to be for us to stay more closely connected to the kids on future getaways. Nothing seemed simple any more.

Our island experience was just one more crazy example of what a dramatic adventure our life had become.

We remembered the days after bringing Carly home from the hospital. She was born screaming. At first, the nurse called it a "Nubaine cry" and assured us that the pain medication Lisa was given during delivery would run through her system in a couple of hours. But four hours later when she was still wailing, another nurse dismissed it suggesting that it often takes ten to twelve hours for babies to settle down after a mom receives pain medication during the late stages of labor. That was Wednesday night. By Thursday morning, Carly had calmed down a little bit but would only suckle fitfully at Lisa's breast. She really only remained quiet and calm for a few minutes at a time when being held in a very specific way that Grandpa discovered and was teaching the rest of us.

At home on Friday Lisa was still struggling to get Carly to nurse and she rarely slept. When Carly did sleep, the slightest sound or movement would wake her. None of it was making sense. We had two children already and so the fear crossed our mind that this might be what severe colic was like. But I think we just hoped it was the lingering aftermath of a chaotic, unexpected labor and delivery.

We had expected Carly to be born by cesarean because of her transverse (crossways) position. The night before the procedure was scheduled, some very dear friends prayed over Lisa surrendering the surgery to God but trusting with us that God could still cause the baby to turn. Labor started three hours later and the baby turned to the proper position shortly after we arrived at the hospital. Our heads were spinning as the plan suddenly changed back to a natural childbirth and, admittedly mentally unprepared, Lisa begged for pain medication without realizing delivery was imminent.

It was into this lack of post-natal bliss that the issue of a severely irritated bottom got inserted. We'd spent most of the night Saturday trying every trick we could think of to soothe her oozing skin but to no avail. Now she was in pain and there was nothing we could do to fix it. In those hours, we became forever convinced that there are few life experiences as emotionally overwhelming as seeing your own child hurting yet knowing of no way to help.

Sunday morning, Lisa sat on the edge of our bathtub sobbing, feeling altogether lost and heartbroken. We wanted to be heading to church bearing that well-known new parent glow and sharing our precious newborn with friends and loved ones. Instead, Carly was screaming again and this time the obvious source was pain from a serious diaper rash. During the night, a bowel movement had eaten through her skin like acid and caused large oozing wounds.

I asked Lisa's mom to go talk with her in the bathroom hoping she might give her some comfort. She knocked on the bathroom door and quietly walked in to find Lisa sitting there on the edge of the bathtub in her pajamas, crying through complete exhaustion. She carefully began to explain. "Dad and I think we should take Alex and Erin with us up to the cabin for a few days. Maybe that would give you and Larry a chance to relax and get some rest so you can try to get on top of things with Carly."

Although we appreciated their compassion, Lisa was overcome with frustration. "I don't know what's wrong with her and I can't make her feel better!" she practically screamed. "This isn't the way it's supposed to be." She was getting really angry. "We're all supposed to be together having fun being a family! I don't want them to go. I don't want you to take my girls away. Why is this happening?"

As we looked back over those early days with Carly, it amazed us that the memories were still so vivid and raw. Disappointment and desperation hung over us like a cloud and it seemed that there was no clearing in sight.

Joseph must have felt this way when his fiancé Mary brought news of her pregnancy in Matthew 1:18-25. I shudder at the agony he must have experienced as he pondered a situation that presented no positive outcomes. If he chose to stay with Mary, he faced living the rest of his life with a woman who had apparently been unfaithful to him, as well as the humiliation that would inevitably come when news of the pregnancy became public. If he chose to end the relationship, it would expose Mary to public disgrace and potentially death by stoning. "This isn't the way it's supposed to be," he must have thought.

The disciple Peter shared a similar reaction in Matthew 16:21-22 after Jesus explained that He must go to Jerusalem to suffer and die at the hands of the religious and political leaders of the time. Peter knew that Jesus was the Messiah, the Son of God. How could it be that the most powerful man in the universe, the conquering King foretold throughout Scripture, the man he had come to love and worship with his entire being, would be killed by mortal men? "This isn't the way it's supposed to be," he must have cried out in his soul.

For several very long weeks after that Sunday in the bathroom, each day looked at least as disturbing as the day before. The diaper rash was worsening, she wasn't nursing well, and she rarely slept. She seemed starved and frustrated, even overwhelmed.

It also got hot. The air conditioning in our new home had not yet been installed. When Carly wasn't sleeping, she was screaming. She seemed hot all the time too but had no fever. She only slept for forty-five minutes at a time in the best of circumstances (which involved someone holding a pacifier in her mouth at all times). If she was asleep, no one dared to move a muscle or make a sound. Just imagine that challenge with a five year-old and a three year-old, especially with no yard to play in outside since our sod had not yet been laid!

After several doctor visits and nurse phone calls, emailed suggestions from friends, and numerous trips to the pharmacy, we had exhausted every rash remedy known to man. As Lisa's dad described it, "she looks like she was dragged on her bottom behind a car going forty miles an hour!" We finally figured out that what worked the best was leaving her bottom open to the air and rinsing it under clean tepid water after every couple of hours. Carly spent all of her time in only an undershirt or entirely naked without diapers on the floor of our family room. The area was layered with bath towels and receiving blankets over plastic trash bags to protect the carpeting.

During a desperate late evening trip to a lactation consultant, even the expert wept out of frustration that she couldn't figure out why Carly wasn't nursing. She simply could not coordinate the suck-swallow thing, something that should be reflexive and intuitive for a baby. Her final suggestion was to express my own milk and give it to Carly in bottles after testing various brands to find the nipple that worked best for her.

So for the next few months, Lisa pumped breast milk seven to nine times a day while I simultaneously fed Carly the milk in bottles. We discovered that enlarging the holes in the nipple with a hot needle allowed Carly to receive trickles of milk without having to suck. She stayed intermittently calm enough to drink if we didn't hold her. Instead, I lay beside her on the floor while holding the bottle and trying to keep myself awake.

In some strange ways it was like a team building and bonding exercise yet I started to feel like Lisa and I were going to go through the rest of our lives on some sort of strange parallel pair of treadmills tending to Carly's needs. One thing was certain, our brains were aching from all the creative problem solving we were doing.

Carly would suck a few times then scream, suck a few times and then scream. Towards the end of a bottle, she might start to doze off. I mastered the art of making a covert and oh-so-gentle switch from the bottle nipple to a pacifier so that she would stay asleep for a little while.

That routine wore on for weeks.

Alex and Erin were big sisters who wanted to help but they quickly grew impatient taking their turns holding the pacifier for Carly. The trick for all of us was keeping ourselves awake or undistracted because, if we so much as twitched, all peace was lost and the crying-feeding-rash management cycle would start all over again. The full cycle — which took between one hour, forty-five minutes and two hours, fifteen minutes — was repeated over and over again twenty-four hours a day until Carly was several months old.

It wasn't until Carly was nearing six or seven months of age that she started to seem more comfortable. Her rash was intermittently under control and she was taking medication for acid reflux. But it was a laborious task keeping ahead of it all. One tiny stool in the middle of the night would trigger a recurrence and have both of us wide awake trying to soothe Carly through a bath and our own tears of frustration.

There were a few bright spots. Our friend Sandy came on two different occasions and spent the night with Carly so that Larry and I could get a few hours of uninterrupted sleep. And there was the day Carly was dedicated to the Lord. No one in the service could hear our pastor praying for her because her screams found no pause even for the Almighty. But by that time, most of our church Body was well aware of the challenges we were facing so they were graciously and sympathetically composed through it all.

Fortunately, Alex and Erin have little memory of those early days. What few memories they do have are of missing opportunities to hold their baby sister and of eating dinner alone at the kitchen table holding their hands over their ears to quiet the sounds of Carly's screaming while Larry and I worked in the adjacent room to get her fed and calmed down.

It wasn't supposed to be this way.

A Different Reality

We celebrated our fifteenth wedding anniversary in my hospital room that summer. The girls brought me a picnic. Afterwards, Lisa and I had plenty of time to hang around in that cold, bland room and ponder our situation. Was it really possible that life had forever changed for us? Was the weekend's collision of our most challenging circumstances just the first in what would become a lifetime of juggling fears and worries, weighty decisions and life-threatening crisis?

Angelman Syndrome and now lymphedema. Neither of these things was curable and each had already shaken our lifestyle to its core. Just a few years before this we had been running a successful consulting business and writing custom training for companies all over the world. We were doing well financially and enjoying the flexibility of self-employment while raising our two little girls.

Our appreciation deepened for people who experienced health conditions that were turning their lives upside down. Nevertheless, we desperately didn't want to be one of "those" people. If this is what it was going to mean to be parents of a handicapped child, then we wanted none of it. And at only thirty-eight years old, I was already feeling like I was living in an old man's body.

I lay in that hospital bed for four days wondering. Would we always feel so consumed by our health issues? Would much of life feel like a lot of waiting around for God to release His healing touch? It certainly looked that way.

Chapter 2:
Navigating the Unknown

Just after the New Year began in 1999, Carly was eight months old. It was apparent to us that she wasn't making expected developmental progress. When the doctor finally agreed that a developmental assessment process should begin, Carly was quickly diagnosed with severe Sensory Integration Dysfunction (SID) and our fears about the significance of her developmental delays were confirmed.

We learned that Sensory Integration Dysfunction is a neurological disorder that involves difficulties with processing information from the five classic senses (vision, hearing, touch, taste, and smell) as well as the senses of movement (vestibular) and position (proprioception). Carly was receiving sensory information normally but her brain was perceiving those messages abnormally. Her interpretation process was disorganized and inefficient.

It made sense. Carly had always responded so unusually to being touched or held. The diagnosis also explained her sensitivity to noise, her odd visual behaviors, her demanding a very specific water temperature during baths, her nursing problems, and so on. Her brain was misinterpreting the signals. When something touched Carly's hand, she reacted as if she had just been caused extreme pain. She startled, pulled back quickly as if she'd been burned, and usually started to shriek uncontrollably. She never relaxed to bear weight on her legs.

If there are good times for getting difficult news, you might say we learned about SID at a good time in the historical understanding of that disorder because new therapies were emerging that were showing great promise in helping children overcome the challenges of sensory disorders. So we were encouraged. It felt good to have some answers and to be developing some proactive plans for a new year. After all, we were people of a proactive nature who were wearing down quickly often having to function in such a reactive mode every day. At the same time, it was more than disconcerting to be introduced to such a foreign world of specialists, philosophies, methodologies, and even vocabulary.

It was like we were learning a whole new language. Besides having Sensory Integration Dysfunction, several other descriptions for Carly were being thrown around — "developmentally delayed," "developmentally disabled," "handicapped," "hypersensitive," "hyposensitive," "high tone," "low tone," and so on. As designers of corporate training programs with a keen interest in the learning process and as writers with a passion for finding the best words to articulate ideas, we wrestled with how to describe Carly's situation to others. We were acutely aware of how the labels we used could influence how people treated her, what they expected of her, and ultimately how they would impact her self confidence and even her ability to learn in the years to come.

After all, we thought, doesn't it make perfect sense that she would have some delays after struggling through all the traumas she'd experienced in those first months? Shouldn't we be very careful about the words we use to describe her situation because we don't want to limit anyone's perception of her potential and inadvertently create a self-fulfilling prophecy? Didn't it make sense that with some meaningful intervention, it would just be a matter of time before she caught back up with her little peers? After all, a diagnosis of Sensory Integration Dysfunction isn't a permanent thing.

Most people experience some degree of difficulty perceiving sensory information in an organized way when they are under stress. For example, my (Lisa's) tolerance for noise during dinner preparation is very low. At that time of day, I'm tired, hungry, and usually in full multi-tasking mode. My brain's information processing abilities are taxed to the limit. I am much more sensitive to the volume of the television in the other room than I am when it is at that same volume another time of the day.

It made sense to us that as Carly's stress was reduced and as we applied therapies to treat her sensitivities to touch and sound, she could make all the progress necessary to catch up. There was every reason to believe that with this new information we could help Carly. We realized it was going to take some time and effort, but we were hopeful if not convinced that she would catch up.

Our neurologist didn't share our optimism. "She is likely to plateau at some point in her development," he flatly said. "Hopefully that will be later rather than sooner. But yes, I do suspect she will plateau."

We left that appointment deflated and really angry. How dare anyone make predictions about our daughter's potential! How dare anyone give up on a child, especially with so little evidence that there is even anything fundamentally wrong! We were appalled.

More Is Better

The only thing left to do was press on with her therapies. We were more determined than ever and felt sure that more therapy could only be better and faster in helping Carly make progress. In addition to the many in-home therapy sessions Carly was receiving every week from the school district, we began tapping into the best clinic-based resources available in the Midwest. Between physical therapy, occupational therapy, speech therapy, and play therapy with a special education teacher, Carly was receiving a minimum of two sessions and sometimes three every day, Monday through Friday. If we weren't at home opening the door to a teacher or therapist toting a bag of exciting toys and therapeutic devices, then we were on the road to specialists at an area clinic or to a highly respected rehabilitation center across town.

The many therapists Carly had were compassionate and hard working. If diligence and commitment were the only measures of success then they were absolute gems. These were some of the most patient, caring, and persistent people you might ever meet. They worked with creativity and compassion to help reduce Carly's sensitivities and move her along on the developmental scale.

Progress was very slow, however, and mostly showed up as gradually improving tolerance. The relative lack of progress specifically related to developmental milestones would have been enough to cause many people to become permanently discouraged. Yet whether they truly believed Carly was capable of significant progress or not, most of these women portrayed cheerfulness and optimism during their interactions with us.

One speech therapist openly expressed her frustration though. She came to me in tears one day at the end of a session with Carly. "I just don't get any response from her at all," she cried in disappointment and frustration. "I'm so sorry. Do you have any ideas about what more I can or should be doing? It's been over six months and I feel like a total failure." I remember thinking that she was supposed to be the expert and how sad it was that she was so ill-equipped by her education and supporting resources that no research was enough to make her efforts fruitful.

We learned so much from those people on many levels. They were the first leaders in helping our family develop a lifestyle that was both focused on capturing opportunities to nurture Carly while also being balanced. Any family living under the near-crushing weight of such life-altering circumstances understands that maintaining balanced attention for all family members and even enjoying a marriage are among the most challenging of issues and the most potentially heartbreaking.

One occupational therapist probably spent as much time mentoring Larry and I through the grieving process and the new complexities of our parenting role as she did hands-on work with Carly. She was a tower of empathy and wisdom for us at a time when we were lost in exhaustion and emotional chaos. We appreciated it then but have grown to appreciate her investment in us even more as the years have passed. We didn't always realize at the time how vulnerable our marriage could have been.

Divorce statistics among families with children who have disabilities are enough to rattle anybody's nerves. We've read about how marriages that go into such an experience already on shaky ground are at extreme risk. On the other hand, reasonably healthy marriages that are faced with such a crisis tend to grow stronger under the weight of the circumstances facing the family. This fact proved true for us. We found ourselves regularly expressing gratitude to God and each other for the marital issues we had wrestled through in the years just before Carly was conceived. God used incredible testing in our marriage to prepare us for what might have been impossible to survive otherwise.

One couple close to us alerted us to two of the most powerful weapons we had against those statistics: our point of focus and prayer. We could focus our attention on the high percentages of marriages that fail or choose to help boost the less favorable ones. We started early claiming the security of our marriage in prayer, asking others to pray for our protection, and making it a priority to nurture what we had.

We owe a debt of gratitude to the many individuals who helped us walk through those early months and years. They affirmed us when we were most shaken in our parental role. They helped us grieve and encouraged us to work together as a team. Probably without even realizing it, they also showed us that some things needed to be done differently.

The Perpetual Drip Between Obstacles and Optimism

There were some frustrating and discouraging encounters with specialists along the way. A substitute physical therapist came into our home one day and worked herself to a sweat with Carly for forty-five minutes. I could see she was very competent as she tried in one session most of the things I'd seen attempted by others in multiple different sessions. Still, she was unable to get Carly to coordinate any of her limbs toward a crawling motion. She was clearly frustrated. "She's quite unusually unresponsive" was the gist of her explanation to me.

Of course, I felt it necessary to point out to her the severity of the tactile sensory issues that Carly had been overcoming in hopes of helping her realize that inordinate patience was required but hope should not be lost. Although she heard me out, she seemed to feel a sense of duty to call me back to reality. Ever so respectfully and gently, she asserted the following conclusion: "You know, Carly may never crawl. In fact, she is not likely to ever walk. I can see you really want to do what's most helpful for your child but, while I know it's hard to accept, you need to focus your goals on something reasonable."

Carly was a tough nut to crack to be sure. By the time she was thirteen months old, her developmental progress could be summarized by one word: tolerance. She was finally a child with some peace. She could not sit independently and was rarely rolling over but she wasn't crying all the time anymore either. She couldn't feed herself or crawl but she would let us hold her and she was a little less resistant to hand-over-hand facilitated play.

Yet with all of the progress Carly had made towards learning some self-soothing skills and tolerance of her surroundings, she was increasingly retreating into a behavior that disturbed and confused us. We called it "hip rocking" because it resembled a side-ways rolling motion that was isolated at her midsection. She would lay face down on the ground with her eyes shut and quite literally zone out while swinging one leg up and down in the air to gain momentum for her side-to-side rolling motion. As she did this, she kept her feet curled tightly inward causing concern that her bones were going to develop abnormally.

Over the months it had become obvious from watching her that the behavior was an attempt to shut out the world and get comfortable. On some level it was a relief to all of us. Carly had found a way to calm herself and we could enjoy some peace and quiet. Yet it was also scary to see her pull away from her surroundings both physically and mentally. The problem was that she could get stuck in the hip-rocking mode for long periods of time. In fact, she persisted in it so insistently at times that it was nearly impossible to get her to stop. She also seemed to be going there compulsively to escape some type of pain or to turn off to the things around her that were overwhelmingly stimulating.

It became increasingly apparent that the behavior was not something to be welcomed but something we desperately needed to resolve and redirect. Every time we saw Carly hip rocking, our hearts would break knowing that we still had a long way to go in understanding the sources of pain and hypersensitivity she was experiencing. Our prayers for healing were most desperate and emotional whenever we saw Carly start to roll over to her tummy, shut her eyes, and go into a zone that seemed to take her farther and farther away from us.

The Birth of a Sibling

Carly's improving level of comfort with her surroundings proved to open critical doors of opportunity for her to develop relationships with her sisters. A most precious Christian woman who did day-care for us in those days was more than instrumental in nurturing those bonds. An extraordinarily patient and creative woman, Toni found ways to help Carly while modeling affectionate interaction between the children. We have an adorable picture of several children standing in a circle around Carly who, as she lay on the floor, looked expectantly at their socks. On Toni's instruction, the kids would take turns wiggling their toes trying to inspire Carly to reach out and touch the soft little curiosities.

We used to chuckle about Erin's role in de-sensitizing Carly to the world around her. Anxious to interact with Carly, Erin would frequently get right up close to Carly's face, nose to nose, and talk to her quite loudly and make silly faces. She was desperate to hold her and cuddle her so the best alternative she could find that wouldn't completely set Carly into fits was to get in her face and create intense affection and silliness through her facial expressions and voice. That gradually became tickling and snuggling. We have at least one memorable photograph of Erin nuzzled up beside Carly who, as usual, was lying on a blanket on the floor. Erin is all grins as if relieved her sister finally likes her.

Since Alex was older, she tended to act more respectfully of Carly's space. So she was thrilled when given the opportunity to hold Carly's bottle and quickly learned to use a gentle voice to calm Carly down when something had upset her.

With all of the therapists in our home both Alex and Erin picked up many ideas about how to play with Carly. The two girls were quickly becoming her best therapists and undeniably talented in their ways. Doesn't every parent feel a warm rush of joy and gratitude to God when they see their children interacting positively with each other? There was a kind of relief to see Alex and Erin discovering ways of relating to Carly. But more than that, they were expressing a level of compassion and wisdom that was mature beyond their years. Carly was captivated by them and they were developing an intuition about how to help her grow. They began to recognize their powerful roles as siblings and we started to discover one of our most powerful tools for unlocking Carly's potential — her sisters.

Carly's true personality was also starting to emerge largely through her relationships with Alex and Erin. She was starting to smile and, when she did, it lit up the room. A couple of years later Erin wrote about Carly in a poem for school saying, "When she smiles, it looks like the sun is glowing on her face."

Developing Her Talents

Carly finally started sitting independently but she was quite unstable and didn't have protective reflexes if she started to fall over. That is to say, she didn't reach out with an elbow, set a hand down, or curve her back to roll down the way other children would. In fact, once she learned how to sit, she seemed to get extremely proficient at keeping herself upright as if she knew that tipping over would be painful without any intuitive appreciation of how to minimize the pain.

She had another reason to begin developing abdominal muscles that would put any infomercial fitness celebrity to shame. Soon after learning to sit, she mastered the skill of sitting with her feet up in the air because she still didn't like her feet to touch anything. This was a skill Carly owned for several years. As a matter of fact, a couple of years down the road she really impressed some friends during a play date at their house.

The kids proudly told their dad they had discovered there was something Carly could do that nobody else could do. "She can keep her feet high in the air when she's sitting on the floor!" they told him when he arrived home from work on day. They tried to demonstrate but found their own abs sorely lacking. They were so proud of Carly and found it really exciting that there was something she could teach them for a change because, by that time, those friends and several other children had become integral members of Carly's therapy team!

All Work But No Work

There were constant meetings and doctor appointments. Telephone conversations, assessments, and team sessions occurred almost every day. And every session had the same tone. There was a sense of urgency and unsettledness that Carly wasn't making much developmental progress. We were setting goals and brainstorming strategies but there was a common thread of frustration that Carly seemed to lack motivation. There were occasional signs of encouragement but no particular milestones were being reached.

The doctors searched for answers as to why Carly wasn't making more progress. A genetic screening had shown no evidence of any abnormalities, serious conditions, or syndromes. We still tended to dismiss her delays to the early traumas of the diaper rash and reflux pain but doubts sometimes haunted us that something deeper and more far-reaching could be involved.

Those first few very hard days had grown into a year of living in a constant state of crisis. This caused us to rely on one another to an extent that we never had before. It felt like it was us against the world. We both felt a deep need for each other to be involved in all of the discovery and strategizing that was required.

Being self-employed gave us the flexibility to attend all of Carly's appointments together. It may not have been the most practical strategy but is was a helpful one for both of us. It proved valuable in helping us engage different ideas or perspectives, answer questions, and stay on a similar page in our processing of the situation.

So if it sounds like we weren't working much that's because we weren't. We were working hard but we weren't working.

We were unable to work. Calls would come but with each one we agonized over how we could possibly meet a client's deadlines. The nature of our business was to work on very aggressive design and development schedules with little flexibility for life's interruptions. Projects came in fits and starts. Being that our clients were among the largest in the world, we felt great pressure to maintain the highest standards of customer service and quality. These companies roll out new products and sales training in weeks not months. We needed to be at the top of our creative game and working with tremendous efficiency.

Lack of sleep, stress, a fragile emotional state…in many cases, we weren't even sure that we were making reasonable decisions about which projects to accept, let alone how to write a reasonable budget. We were utterly consumed with Carly's inability to sleep and her chronic pain and screaming episodes.

Only the rarest job had a deadline or level of simplicity that felt conducive to the unpredictable sort of schedule we were keeping. As our cash flow was stretched and the new mortgage payments were increasingly challenging to make, we began to tap into our investments and, ultimately, our retirement savings to pay the bills.

We also learned some hard lessons about living too optimistically. Our income had been very strong for several years, even though a consulting business often experiences significant payment fluctuations. It certainly wasn't like the days of having both of our paychecks automatically deposited every two weeks. So when we bought the new house, we purchased several new furnishings on credit confident that our income was sound though sporadic.

Our new, deeper sense of teamwork as a couple had come at a steep price. What little of ourselves that had not been poured out during the crises of Carly's early life we willingly poured out as we pursued healing and wholeness for her. Our finances took a back seat. It is a trade we would willingly make again. But it was also a trade that would have consequences for years to come.

Turning Point or Breaking Point?

We were rounding the corner on eighteen months since Carly was born and it seemed like all of life had radically changed yet, in many ways, it felt like time was standing still. We had prayed countless prayers for healing. We had spent many Sundays at the altar receiving prayer. We had claimed the power of Jesus' shed blood over Carly knowing that the ultimate victory of whatever was interfering with her development was in the spiritual realm where God alone would fight the battle. We even ventured way out of our usual comfort zone to visit a healing room where people with spiritual gifts of healing would anoint Carly with oil and pray for a special release of the power of the Holy Spirit in her life and body. Lots of heartache, lots of therapeutic activity, lots of prayer. Some progress had been experienced, but lots of things seemed the same as the day Lisa sat on the side of that tub.

Our life was extremely full and yet we felt very alone. It's a sad paradox that people in all kinds of circumstances experience — being surrounded by people and activity can even magnify the feeling. Loneliness, we were learning, is a pervasive part of living within a life-changing health crisis. I (Larry) describe it as a "sensation" because it is more of an inner experience than a description of outward reality. We were surrounded by people who loved us. Many had quite literally even helped take care of us in many respects. Yet the inner experience of feeling quite alone was often overwhelming.

Some physical costs from the strain were also emerging. I was diagnosed with high blood pressure and found myself in a perpetual state of melancholy, which was not normal for me. As we discussed the situation with our family physician, he suggested trying an anti-depressant "just for a season." In the end, the medications did not make a significant difference but a sleep apnea was discovered. That was interesting. What could I tell a doctor who tried to assure me that a c-pap would help me sleep better. It was going to take a lot more than that at my house!

The scenario unfolding with Carly caused mixed reactions among our friends and family. This took us a little by surprise and sometimes left us retreating into ourselves. Perhaps understanding, empathy, and compassion were what we craved most. Our days (and nights) were very intense and there seemed to be no end in sight. A few of our friends and family appreciated how challenged we were yet even those people struggled to know how they could really help. Others gradually grew distant. We all know the hesitation of asking even a casual, "how are you" because we aren't sure how to respond if we get the honest answer. Some of our friends noticeably closed the door and moved on.

There is no disputing we were a demanding couple to be friends with on practical, spiritual, and emotional levels. We were facing some of life's harshest realities when one friend suggested to Lisa that things always seemed to revolve around her. She couldn't accept that. Ouch! But you know what? In many ways, that was true. After all, life isn't perfect for anybody. Yet the process of learning to bear our burdens gracefully often doesn't come quickly either.

We spent so much time in "survival mode" that we had come to praise the Lord daily for the friends and family who dug their heels into a relationship with us and stuck it out even when they were very tired of our "woe is us" moments. Those were the cherished ones who recognized that our burdens were their burdens just as theirs were among ours. There was no guaranteed escape from hardship for us any more than they could choose to escape from a relationship with us just because our life was pretty draining for everybody. In it for the long haul, they saw loving us and sticking by our side as both God-given responsibility and Divine blessing. What a gift!

We were living life in a tug-of-war between wanting and needing to retreat into the relative comfort and safety of our routine and sensing the need to press outward. At least we were learning what we could expect at home. But the relentlessness of it all often inspired us to want to run away to anything else but what faced us there. So to any extent we could manage, we poured into sports and school activities with the other girls as well as church activities. Our weekly family small group meetings with worship, fellowship, and Bible

Study were our greatest source of refreshment. Those brothers and sisters in the Lord became our anchor.

Carly's hip rocking was a metaphor for the kind of autopilot we were on. We were at risk of staying stuck there without a sense of vision. So realizing how profoundly God uses people who are willing to live with transparency was affirming and purpose-filling for us.

That was a key turning point. Because even though we still didn't know where the story was going or where it was going to end, we were growing to sense God's intensifying promptings to live the story "out loud." Living our story somewhat publicly (often much more publicly than we were comfortable with) was going to be what got us through — and what would help get some others through. That was going to be one of God's economies in the whole thing, one of the ways he was going to use Carly's journey and us. That's what propelled us. It's how God spurred us on, refreshed us, and filled us with renewed energy each day.

Our vision of God's plan was still more vague than we would have liked but having a sense that in some small way His purposes were being fulfilled in and through us gave us inspiration. We were going to need that Divine inspiration because what lay just around the corner in grandma's mailbox and what we heard in one doctor's phone call would soon turn our lives on a whole new end.

Our Season In Community

…God has combined the members of the body

and has given greater honor to the parts that lacked it,

so that there should be no division in the body,

but that it's parts should have equal concern for each other.

If one part suffers,

every part suffers with it;

if one part is honored,

every part rejoices with it.

Now you are the body of Christ,

And each one of you is a part of it.

I Corinthians 12:24b-27

Chapter 3:
Empowered to Action

It was like any ordinary evening at our house when the phone rang. Alex was probably playing the piano. Erin dancing. Larry, working in the basement or feeding Carly. I (Lisa) was either washing dishes, folding laundry, or trying to coax fifteen-month old Carly out of hip rocking or disinterest in toys.

Hearing my dad's voice first on the telephone line was unusual and he got straight to the point. "Your mom wants to talk to you. She's been learning about something that could be very helpful for Carly. You'll want Larry on the phone to hear this too." My dad had a curious tone, as if he was anxious to get right to the point yet gentle as if not wanting to trigger fear. As their message unfolded it became clearer that I was hearing optimism mixed with guardedness. They didn't want us to feel pushed into something but they clearly felt a strong conviction about what they were sharing.

Never since we were married had any of our parents made recommendations related to our personal decisions. Larry and I are both fortunate to have parents who have great respect for our privacy and choices. So we remember listening with great curiosity to hear what had gotten mine so charged up.

My mom began explaining. "About a month ago, we got a flyer in the mail from a family down the street. They were asking for volunteers to help with a special program for their disabled son. Because of Carly's challenges, my heart went out to them and I regretted being unable to make the weekly commitment they needed. Then I ran into my neighbor out at our mailboxes last week and found out she was helping them. She needed a substitute and that seemed like a good way for me to help given my inconsistent schedule." My mom barely paused for breath before continuing.

"I spent at least two hours with that little boy, Judd, and his mom last week. His story is a miracle. Within a few hours of his birth, his parents were told he would remain in a vegetative state requiring intensive care all of his life. They were urged to begin immediately locating an institution where he could live. The brain matter connecting the two hemispheres of the little boy's brain was missing. She called it abbreviated corpus callosum. His parents refused to accept what the doctors told them and they brought him home. His mother quit a very good job and they started an intensive home therapy program that she leads. They've had dozens of helpers coming and going every day. Judd is three years old now and already creeping on his hands and knees. He is even reading at a first grade level!"

My mom barely paused. Larry and I sat at separate phones listening quietly amazed, curious about what this family had done but overwhelmed by the myriad of thoughts, emotions, and questions that were already flooding our hearts and minds. Despite all the reasons to prompt hesitation within us, there was something about the momentum of my mom's enthusiasm and the truly inspirational nature of that family's story that helped us resist the urge to dismiss it all too quickly.

My dad started adding details explaining things he learned about the brain since reading about Judd's program. He emphasized that cross-pattern crawling movements make a fundamental contribution to the stimulation of new brain connections. He explained that those movements could be simulated through exercises even before a child was independently mobile. He talked about the benefits of that kind of input for a person's brain as well as how the movements could even have a life-saving impact. The movement would be strengthening for the torso and lungs of a child who would typically be vulnerable to serious health issues including scoliosis or respiratory infections like pneumonia. He also talked about the critical role that oxygenation of the brain plays in healing.

I was almost breathless listening. Larry and I remember wondering and praying, "Lord, what does all of this mean? Why does this feel so unsettling and yet powerful? Does Carly really need something this radical? We don't have time to do all this research! How could we possibly recruit the help of dozens of people to accomplish something like that! Oh Holy Spirit, you're going to have to make your will as clear as day to us on this one!"

There was another thing unexpectedly unsettling about that phone call. It was almost nauseating to consider Carly in anything close to the same category as Judd. Yet God seemed to be easing us into the realization that Carly was falling further and further behind developmentally. Her function was that of a three to six month old on her best days. There was no denying she needed to make radical progress. And if radical improvements were going to be made, radical measures would need to be taken.

A New Vision

Up to this point, I (Larry) had been of the mind that doing as much therapy as possible was the best we could offer Carly. Yet the more reading Lisa did, the more we began to appreciate that the methods themselves really did matter. Frequency and repetition, just teaching and re-teaching skills, wasn't going to be enough. Activity alone didn't guarantee fruitfulness, especially when one considered the amount of time we were spending just driving from session to session in the car. We were challenged to reconsider that the very specific nature as well as the intensity of the input she received was going to be at least as important as how often that input was repeated.

I vividly remember Lisa reading to me during car rides and in bed at night. It was amazing stuff and I quickly sensed it would be meaningful for Carly. It was empowering to recognize that if God created our bodies with the ability to repair and heal, then Carly's brain had exciting ability to organize, recover, and develop with great potential.

We lay in bed one night praying together that God would show us what to do. We both got the message that we should start implementing the things that seemed most immediately doable, keep praying, and wait for the Lord on the rest. Lisa made this journal entry on September 16ᵗʰ, 1999:

> Lord Jesus, give us a window into Carly's spirit (her heart, mind, potential, preferences) that will make us the best possible parents to her. Open it wide so that Larry and I have fresh and clear perspective about what will help her. Shine into each of us as an energy that will help Carly blossom and explore but will help us even stay awake to see it happen!

We were depending on our belief that God would make His will clear and that when it was clear we would need to promptly and obediently follow it. But when it was unclear, we were to wait patiently but attentively.

And so we began. We started by working on strategies to give Carly more time on her tummy. By now she was rolling from front to back but could not and would not go to or stay face down. We learned this was one of the most developmentally healthy positions for a baby to play in.

Lisa's mom fashioned a vest for Carly like one that Judd wore. When she went to a hardware store for PVC supplies, even the hardware store staff got excited about helping our little girl. They designed and built Carly a set of anti-roll "wings" that fastened to the back of the zipped vest Grandma had sewn. Carly wasn't impressed. It was impossible for her to get into her face-up comfort zone yet we could quickly see that there were many benefits for her and for us.

At the same time, I had begun building an adjustable slide. It was designed to help her recognize the connection between her own movements and forward motion. The degree of incline was adjusted to ensure that any wiggling she did would result in her sliding downward toward a prized cuddly toy. I had fun building it. It wasn't a matter of buying some magic gadget or medication that would just fix everything. This rather cumbersome piece of equipment became the first significant tangible way we could help Carly.

Having her wear the winged vest while on the slide proved to maximize her opportunities and increase her independence. It really was an amazing set of circumstances that came together. It was both fascinating and affirming that we were on the right track.

While we were experimenting with the slope of the slide and trying to manage the "friction factor," we wondered how to go to the next level. We had connected with both local and national resources who had complimentary philosophies and methods and we were gaining vision about what to do. But some of the activities that would help Carly required a three-person team. We still needed God to show us where that help was going to come from.

Lisa shared our growing vision with a few friends in her weekly women's Bible Study group and asked them to pray. Three of those ladies walked up to her after class that day, looked her squarely in the eye, and told her in no uncertain terms "you and Larry need to tell this church that you need their help." One of them added, "You need to stand up in front of our congregation and tell them what Carly needs. You need to give God the opportunity to show them what it means to minister to each other."

Lisa's study leader insisted, "I'm also going to give you a few minutes at the beginning of our next class to tell all of the ladies what you need."

Life is Not to Be Lived Alone

I shuddered when Lisa told me what those ladies had said. The last thing we wanted to do was make a general request in public about our need for help. Would people think less of us for not handling things on our own? Would they think us selfish? Why should our situation be given special attention? There are all kinds of needs in a church at any given time. Would they understand that it wasn't money we needed? We needed manpower and prayer power. Would they judge our strategies? And worst of all: What if they said "no?"

There were, in fact, some people concerned that if we were allowed to stand up during a service and ask for help, many others would expect the same kind of opportunity. Fortunately, we had advocates who challenged that notion by suggesting that one of the primary functions of the Body of Christ is to minister to its members. Those women from Bible Study raised the beautiful challenge that serving each other in need was exactly what the Church should be about. Maybe we should let people stand up and ask for help more often! They went so far as to tell me our situation might be one the Lord wanted to use to remind the Body about what they are to be for each other. Scary. And humbling.

A date was set for us to give testimony of our need during two services in early February. The week before we stood in front of our congregation, Lisa sent an email to family and friends. Our February 11, 2000 message read:

> We're close to wrapping up a long process of research and prayer that has brought us to a new and exciting point in helping Carly learn. While studying much about the connections between brain development and crawling, we have decided to begin an intensive, home-based program…very structured…five hours a day, six days a week.
>
> We have spent the last month addressing various medical opinions about Carly's vision and have also completed a four-hour long evaluation for the neurophysiological program. It is totally fascinating stuff.
>
> In the meantime, Carly really seems ripe for learning. Having glasses has completely opened up her world. It's just nothing short of a miracle. (Even we are amazed when we look back and compare pictures of her vacant smile just last fall. It's like night and day.) In addition, we have been working hard on oral-facial massage which has improved her oral muscle tone and control to the extent that she is becoming much more verbal and making a wider variety of sounds. Still no words but great improvements in her

eating and babbling. At twenty-one months of age she is finally on one hundred percent table food! Ahhhh.

Having her spend more time face down on the floor working on crawling has given her cognitive development a boost. We think she is starting to respond to more of our words. The ones we are confident she now understand are "drink," "spoon," "no," "come," "stand up," "dance," "push," "kiss," and "bye-bye." I can't tell you how exciting it is for Larry and I to feel we can finally begin to communicate with her on some level. It brings tears to our eyes every evening at the dinner table to hear her "mmmmmm" when she wants us to give her another bite of dinner. (She is not yet feeding herself so it's wonderful to hear indication that she wants more.)

So we are in an overwhelming but hopeful time of transition. In the next two weeks we are fully launching a home program. This is where we will especially need your prayers. Implementing the program at home is more than what one family can do by themselves. VOLUNTEERS come to the home for one hour a week and assist with activities and exercises. No experience is needed. Larry or I will train them. Volunteers can also help shop, cook, clean, or give Larry or me time to work or have time for ourselves.

Please pray with us for the following:

- That volunteers (and a volunteer coordinator) will be provided
- That Carly will adjust quickly and benefit from the program in a significantly positive way
- That we will keep all the balls in the air and our time balanced appropriately between our kids, our work, our marriage, and our personal quiet times
- That in this hectic schedule, people will see God's grace and gratefulness in us, that our family will minister into the lives of those we encounter just as deeply as they will be ministering into ours

Only the Lord will give us the strength, wisdom, people support, and healing that will allow Carly to continue to grow joyfully into who she is. I can't emphasize enough how much we love Carly. That has nothing to do with her achievements or lack of them. Our concern is simply to give Carly the best possible opportunities to become who Jesus wants her to be — whatever that involves.

Your prayers carry us. THANK YOU SO MUCH! God bless you.

The boldness of our efforts to publicize our needs still felt awkward but we had an increasing sense that this was no longer just our own vision but an act of obedience. God had made Himself clear and given us a great peace that we were headed in the direction He'd pointed. It was time to throw caution to the wind and pull out all the stops. We were on a mission and ready for anything.

God Did Immeasurably More than All We Asked or Imagined

Larry did a terrific job of explaining our hearts. I (Lisa) stood holding Carly beside him at the front of our sanctuary that day. Tears fell quietly down his cheeks and I could see his hands hung trembling at his sides but he never seemed taller and stronger to me than he did in that moment.

We didn't want people to come unless they really felt called by the Holy Spirit. He explained that it wasn't a matter of having special gifts in this situation but more important that people had a passion. We needed people who really wanted to be there. And we were sure that God would provide enough help that no one would have to come because they felt guilt or pressure.

The response was immediate and overwhelming. Larry and I stood trembling and crying in front of our congregation that February morning and by noon had about a dozen commitments. To our relief and surprise, both friends and strangers were offering us one hour a week. We had never been more acutely aware of the preciousness of people's time or more grateful for the gift of it.

We were struck by how joyfully people came. One woman came up behind me and touched my elbow as I spoke with another eager volunteer. It was obvious her heart ached to help but she admitted concern. "I had a stroke about a year ago and I am still weak on one side. I don't know if there is something I will be able to do but I would very much like to help."

A widow from my Bible Study offered to be our volunteer coordinator. My "Wednesday morning cheerleaders" sent affirming and excited glances our way many times that day from across the fellowship areas of the church as we stopped in conversation with people who were signing up to help or apologizing for their lack of availability but interest in praying for us. A couple of people even admitted to having already prayed for quite some time acknowledging that they could tell we were having a great deal of difficulty with Carly but hadn't wanted to say anything.

March 20, 2000 was the first day. Volunteers started coming and going in pairs on the hour. They checked themselves in at a notebook on our kitchen table, went down to our basement and washed their hands, then came around the corner to find the previous group working on the program activities.

There were women and men, old and young. There were retired couples, home schooled children, neighbors, cousins, friends of friends, and many, many loved ones from our church.

Those hours were busy, often chaotic times moving from one activity to another. Amid encouraging conversation, there was also much brainstorming about how one activity or another could be done more effectively. For example, Carly was supposed to bear weight on her hands and knees for two minutes four times a day. How in the world were we going to get this child to put her hands on the floor, let alone hold them there and bear weight? This was the child whose hands were so sensitive to touch that jerked away as if burned when given something to hold. She wouldn't touch a single thing without screeching tears of pain or frustration.

A retired man from our church graciously set to work building a carpet board that was to be used with Velcro gloves to keep her hands down. But from the very first test, Carly was entirely too quick and strong for the gloves. In only seconds her hands were high in the air as she grimaced and howled. The gloves remained firmly stuck on the carpeting. On to Plan B.

Before too long I was straddling Carly from behind, both of us sitting on our haunches with knees bent underneath. Someone else was kneeling in front of her holding her hands flat on the floor. I had to put a solid grip around each of her elbows to prevent her from bending her arms to wriggle away. A third helper had the mighty task of reading books, blowing bubbles, and singing to entertain Carly and distract her from her escape efforts. All the while this human pretzel took shape, a fourth helper sat on the couch using a cooking timer to keep track of time and noting the duration on the day's checklist. What a scene it was!

Our goal was two minutes. Our first attempt lasted about fifteen seconds. Maintaining our collective strength and composure for this crazy pose was almost more than any of us could bear. It was often impossible to hear the storyteller through the laughter and giggles. But with each attempt, her tolerance improved and was measurable in seconds. The first time we made it all the way through to the alarm sound of the timer, you would have seen at least three grown adults drop to the floor in exhaustion shouting praises of accomplishment while Carly sat half bewildered by the fuss and mostly satisfied that she was finally free.

All that creativity and wrestling was proving itself fruitful. Everyone marveled as the days unfolded. Every struggle and success was a fascinating reminder of God's amazing creation. Each of us was in awe to consider what miracles lie behind every subtle, often unnoticed, layer of development in a child. We were no longer taking anything about how children learn and develop for granted. Grandparents helping with Carly's program were admitting they now saw the miracles of their own grandchildren with new eyes and appreciation. We were all learning a deeper respect for God's design of the human body and appreciating even the most subtle signs of God's powerful hand at work in His creation.

In so many ways Carly's progress was immediate and overwhelming, far more than we ever imagined we would witness so quickly. With every day that passed, sometimes with each hour and shift change, we were noticing something new in her function emerging. There was such an excitement in the process that as each new pair of volunteers came every sixty minutes, there were hugs and stories exchanged about all that was happening.

It became obvious very quickly that we needed to keep a diligent record of the miraculous work God was doing. From a practical perspective, we needed to resist getting chatty and stay focused on our work. We needed to find an efficient way to share news so the momentum of Carly's therapies could be maintained throughout the day. We also needed a way to share the excitement with all those who couldn't be with us but had committed to pray us through.

But it was more than all that. We never wanted to forget. We felt compelled to celebrate every detail. We needed a way to keep track of the highlights and challenges so there would always be a way to look back and remember God's faithfulness to us on the journey.

So at the end of that first week of Carly's precious program, we started emailing weekly updates to family and friends. Sitting down to write each one of these updates felt like our process of making a rock pile at the Jordan River. If we were really in a process of crossing over to a "promised land" of sorts, then each deliberate note we made recognizing what God was doing would be a remembrance and celebration to look back on for generations.

What quickly became known as the "Carly Updates" went to dozens of people who would continue to stand soundly as our prayer warriors for many years to come.

On March 28, 2000, we reflected on that first week together:

> On Saturday, we finished our first full week of Carly's program that involved twenty-four volunteers! About fourteen people attended the Information Meeting last Saturday. It was a very busy week of training and learning and practicing. I think everyone was encouraged to know how much they are contributing to Carly's development, and they truly are! Many have asked us to publicly and

regularly share the changes we are seeing in Carly as well as prayer requests. So here goes for this week…

Praises/changes for the week of March 20:

- Carly loves log rolling on a blanket and by Wednesday was reflexively using her limbs to control her movements.
- After receiving some support, Carly is able to support herself on hands and knees for about ten seconds (two weeks ago, she would not even keep her hands on the floor).
- Carly visually and tactilely (with right hand especially) explored a bowl of rice — this is a significant improvement in motor skill, visual attending, and level of curiosity especially considering she rarely uses her right hand for anything.
- Carly's tolerance for cross-patterning is increasing every day (we're up to two minutes without strong objections).
- MOST IMPORTANT—Carly is starting to develop a pincer grasp on her right hand so she has started picking up chunks of food and putting them in her mouth independently. In addition, she is picking up a fork and putting it in her mouth which also involves having to turn her wrist to fit the fork squarely in her mouth (this is HUGE).
- Praise God with us for our neighbor, Michelle, who is supplying us with one meal EVERY WEEK (what an incredible blessing).

Prayer requests:

- We still need twenty-five more commitments of one hour per week as well as many who would be willing to fill in occasionally as substitutes.
- We send thanks from the bottom of our hearts for each and every one of you. May you be abundantly blessed for sharing yourselves and your time with us.

*"Because of your partnership in the gospel from the **first day** (March 20), we are confident of this, the Lord God who*

began a good work in Carly will carry it on to completion
until the day of Christ Jesus."
PHILIPPIANS 1:5-6 (Our paraphrase and emphasis)

Those powerful days grew in number as we continued to discover the value of giving Carly very specific and meaningful input. Her program was revised or adjusted often as her responses became more appropriate and mature. Much of her progress was nothing short of stunning to all of us watching God's handiwork.

Admittedly, it was tempting at times to forget the power of all the prayer going on behind the scenes. After all, there was more energy, attention, and expertise being poured into this child's life than most challenged children could ever hope to receive. It was a lesson for all of us in remembering that no matter how much human effort and wisdom were poured into the situation, God was ultimately in control of the outcome. No matter what else was going on, prayer was the most fundamental and powerful thing anyone was doing. God alone stood in authority over any progress or healing that was made.

Over the next several weeks we observed many exciting signs of progress and answered prayers. Numerous examples were highlighted in the "Carly Updates." Among them were these:

- Her stamina is dramatically increasing as she's doubled her distance with assisted crawling over two weeks. She can now go forty feet in five minutes.
- Carly independently held Mike's finger during the positive gravity exercise.
- The resistance on her right side has dramatically reduced since Doris sensed the Lord prompting her to pray specifically for that. Knowing nothing about Doris' prayers, several people commented about how much more cooperative Carly was on that side in the hours and days following my discussions with Doris.
- We think Carly sometimes says "again" during one of her vision activities. Larry heard her call him "da da" a few times one evening.

- Hannah taught all of us a back-rub rhyme that Carly loves!
- Serena has been baby-sitting the last three Saturdays so we could get a date together away from home. Each evening has been **fabulous!**
- Carly said "KICK" while kicking macaroni off of mom's hand today. (Mom and two volunteers gaped in astonishment then erupted in applause!)
- Carly's reflexes are developing. She grabbed to hold on with her hands this week during spinning—a spontaneous reaction we consider a **huge** accomplishment!
- Her curiosity is emerging which gives us more ways to motivate her. And she's growing to love all the attention of the many people coming and going. At twenty-three months old, she's starting to giggle for social games like peek-a-boo.
- Carly will now reach for things while sitting on her bench. When we strategically place a high-interest item on the floor near her feet, we can now lure her into bending over to pick things up. Just weeks ago, the process of bending over required so much balance and strength that as she leaned forward, she would startle back with great alarm.
- Daddy figured out part of the reason why Carly may be waking up at night. Her feet are too hot in the slippers she's been wearing! Go figure. We've **all** been sleeping better this week.
- Last week we asked you to pray for motivation in assisted crawling and this week was much better! Carly enjoyed crawling to her image in a mirror and started bringing her right knee up on her own for the first time. (Her Physical Therapist was amazed and greatly encouraged!)
- While filming a video Easter card (progress report) for the grandparents, Carly checked the reflection in the fireplace glass with other things she saw in the room. Her recognition that the image was a reflection is amazing testimony of cognitive function that simply was not there only weeks ago.

- Standing is not so scary for Carly most of the time now. During her sitting and standing exercise at the bench, she is doing much better with the transition. Although she still relies on support from someone, she will bend at the knee and bear some weight cooperatively.
- After six weeks of program, everyone is commenting, "Carly is so much more aware and curious about what's going on around her…lots more reaching and exploring…looks two inches taller!" All the hanging and stretching does seem to have loosened her muscles and joints so that she quite literally is about two inches taller than she was in March.

As the weeks and months went by, we continued to be awed by the many hours of time that dozens of people were giving each week to help Carly grow and get well. I never expected to have so much to write so each week I vowed to make our updates more brief. Yet every Saturday afternoon when Larry and I sat down to share reflections on the week, we were overwhelmed by the subtle but amazing progress the Lord was revealing in Carly every single day! We wondered what we could ever say to anyone that would express how humbled we were, how hopeful we were growing, how loved we felt.

In the meantime, we were also seeing God's hand all over the logistics of schedules, the relationships that were developing and the faith that was growing in the community surrounding Carly's program. The remaining shifts were quickly filling with new volunteers. Without exception people came enthusiastic, optimistic, and always with encouragement for us.

We were frequently amazed by how many details God would sort out for us. For example, one morning I called our volunteer coordinator asking her to cancel a couple of shifts because Carly would be at a doctor's appointment. She would respond in amazement that she had just received two calls from volunteers needing substitutes for the same time period. Or I would just be feeling an overwhelming need for a break but not wanting to disappoint any of our very enthusiastic volunteers.

And then a call would come in that someone was sick or needed to reschedule a shift.

We also sensed God's protection of our health. With so little sleep and so many people coming and going, we were on prayerful guard against picking up any illness going around. There was also concern for our volunteers, many of whom were retired men and women who could be vulnerable if they became sick through their time with us. Everyone was asked to wash their hands at the beginning and end of their shifts and to get a substitute if they were ill. But only by the grace of God did the next few years pass with very few sick days for all those involved.

The "Carly Updates" continued. The week of Carly's second birthday I wrote:

> Carly's belly crawling is fast improving in form. About two weeks ago she started using her right leg (instead of dragging her torso using only her arms) and now she is often bringing her left leg into the process too! Even better, she sometimes pushes and pulls so hard that her belly will rise briefly off the floor. Ben and Diane worked hard with her crawling on Friday afternoon which set the tone for more independent movement than usual this weekend.

Singing with the Angels

One of our core activity sequences involved simulating a cross-pattern crawling motion. It took three people to help move Carly's body through a particular range of motion exercise in methodical rhythm. I led the exercise with two volunteer helpers most of the time. But if we were short a person, Larry could be pulled from his work in the adjacent room to step in and help.

Certainly the rhythmic nature of the movements was enough to inspire any group of song-loving souls but when we were mindlessly repeating an otherwise boring routine multiple times a day, several preschool songs and traditional hymns with 4-4 timing came to mind. Carly relaxed to our groovin' voices quite nicely. "Row Row Row Your Boat" and "Amazing Grace" kept her well entertained while the rest of us took joy in the harmonies. No choir robes were needed here. The smiles on our faces and the tiny beads of sweat on our brows were enough to make us glow for Jesus!

At the end of the exercise, Carly would roll up to sitting and grin at us as if she were truly grateful for the help. Many months into the process she seemed to imitate one of the women who clapped her hand on top of the padded cross-patterning table. And so began a little game of tapping in turns that frequently celebrated the conclusion of a good cross-patterning session. I'm not sure what thrilled us more, the sparkle in Carly's eyes that was non-existent before the days of her program or the fact that she was interacting on such a meaningful level in a social game.

One day at the end of her shift, one of the women handed me a small pile of recipe cards on which she had written about a dozen Scriptures. She and several other women had paraphrased them and were praying specifically for Carly. Among them:

Carly shall run and not be weary; she shall walk and not faint OR become tired.
ISAIAH 40:3

Carly shall walk in all the ways which the Lord her God has commanded that she may live and that it may go well with her and that she may live long in the land which she shall possess.
DEUTERONOMY 5:33

Lord, we want our eyes to be opened.
MATTHEW 22:33

We set our minds on those things that gratify the Holy Spirit.
ROMANS 8:5B

God didn't give us a spirit of timidity, but of power and of love and of calm and well-balanced mind and discipline and self-control.
2 TIMOTHY 1:7

I will not leave you without support.
HEBREWS 13:5

By His stripes we are healed!
1 PETER 2:24

The devil comes to steal, kill and to destroy. I came so that everyone might have life and have it to its fullest.
JOHN 10:10

Scripture often guided the whole group of us. During that first summer of Carly's program, a financial gift allowed us to hire a teen-aged girl to lead some of the program so I could get a break and more work done. She came one morning admitting that she'd been struggling with Carly's resistance to some activities and was feeling guilty about challenging her so much. But while she was journaling, God showed her Hebrews 12. Her eyes grew bright as she shared the passage with me.

No discipline seems pleasant at the time but painful. Later on, however, it produces a harvest of righteousness and peace for those who have been trained by it. Therefore, strengthen your feeble arms and weak knees. Make level paths for your feet, so that the lame may not be disabled, but rather healed.
HEBREWS 12:11-13

The original context of the passage had to do with sin. In this case, we understood that God was reminding us that hard work and training are not always enjoyable, but often necessary and worthwhile.

Later that day, each volunteer joined us in a commitment to memorize those two key verses together. With great expectations, we claimed the promise for developmental progress as well as spiritual fruit.

Chapter 4:
Watching in Wonder

Those hours of program time were fast becoming powerful times of bonding. We were bonding with volunteers. Volunteers were bonding with each other. Everyone was bonding with Carly.

As a mom, I was experiencing a special answer to prayer through my new sense of connection to her. As the fatigue and raw emotions of those early months had worn on, I had felt a scary lack of attachment to Carly. I didn't sense the kind of bond I'd had with my older girls and I was worried about what a challenge it could be for me to stay engaged in hours of child-like play throughout her program activities every day.

While I had always loved young children and had a knack for teaching them, my attention span was short for such things. After all, I had not even spent long devoted hours with my other children as a mom with a full time career. By the time Alex and Erin were two years old, they were quite able to keep themselves entertained while I kept busy in the periphery. As a result I found myself privately begging God to grow a special connection between Carly and me and develop my attentiveness for things of interest to her.

My silent prayer had been answered. Carly was becoming more engaging and I was growing more fascinated with her than ever. In fact, my prayer quickly changed into a prayer for grace. There was encouraging progress and momentum, but I was impatient and wanted more. I didn't want her to become the latest "performance problem" I would solve that would validate me or give me a sense of purpose. So my next stage of praying became "Lord, remind me constantly that this process is not about me. Show me how to take joy in each moment with Carly and leave the results in Your hands alone."

I received an email from our neighbor, Diane, one afternoon that described a child with a syndrome that involved seizures and an unusually happy, even excitable, demeanor. Diane was a dig-around kind of mom. I appreciated that because I wanted information but preferred to stay as focused as possible on getting program done. Having a handicapped child of her own, Diane knew well how to navigate the Internet and medical research.

Larry and I read the website link Diane had provided and marveled that anyone would connect Carly with the description: "frequent laughter/smiling; apparent happy demeanor; easily excitable personality." It was a miracle that Carly was finally considered a rather happy and content child. How ironic that someone would consider Carly a "fit" for this type of diagnosis considering the chaotic and miserable nature of her first year. The prognosis was grim for someone with Angelman Syndrome, the condition outlined on the website, and so we took further comfort in the fact that Carly had never had a seizure. (More than eighty percent of people with Angelman Syndrome had seizures by thirty years old.) We were also grateful that genetic testing done when Carly was only a few months old had all been normal.

Diane's research inspired me to poke around looking at a handful of other syndromes and, though the process was interesting to me, it was mostly just depressing and nothing seemed meaningful anyway. So I determined to spend my time undistracted by trying to find a name for what she might have and simply press on with the therapeutic tools God was facilitating.

It was the beginning of October 2000 and Carly was two and a half years old. My parents had just come into town and were thrilled to see all the progress they had been reading about and praying for. So none of us was prepared for the moment during dinner one evening when I looked up from my plate to see Carly drooping oddly in her high chair. She was staring blankly at her chest and drooling. One hand twitched ever so slightly and she was kicking her leg.

Larry and I locked eyes in fear while one of us spoke the word we were both thinking. "Seizure?"

The thought of calling an ambulance barely crossed our minds because we knew the fastest access to experience with seizures was right out our back door. "I'm calling Diane," I gasped as I ran for the phone.

Diane wasn't home but her husband, Perry, was on his way up the steps of our deck. His first look at Carly confirmed our fear. "Yup, that's a seizure," he said sadly. "Call 911."

Each of us cried in shock as we waited for help to come. Larry and I held Carly's limp body that was pulsing with increasing intensity as we sobbed out a desperate prayer. Alex and Erin clung to grandma wide-eyed while quiet tears streamed down my mom's face. The sense of something very ominous held its grip on the room.

Diane met us at the Emergency Room that night. She stood respectfully in the distance offering quiet support and wisdom. When the doctors recommended a next step, we would often turn simultaneously to look at Diane with question marks in our eyes. Sometimes she simply nodded reassuringly as if to say, "It's okay, that's what they need to do." Other times, she would gently touch my arm and prompt me with an important question to ask. "Ask them what they're giving her."

Almost an hour after the ordeal had begun, Carly's body was finally calm and she was sleeping peacefully. Larry and I were exhausted, relieved, confused, and very anxious. What could all of this possibly mean?

Diane delicately made us aware that a more specialized genetic test for Angelman Syndrome could be done while Carly was admitted to the hospital. So the next day, we asked our neurologist if such diagnostics could be considered. "That would be appropriate," he said simply then added, "It will take several weeks to learn the results." Blood workup. A spinal tap. A CAT scan. No answers.

That was not to be the last we heard of seizures, nor was it the end of the discussion of Angelman Syndrome. I was busy doing program one morning three weeks later when the neurologist called and indicated he had test results for Angelman Syndrome. With immediate alarm, I asked Larry to go to another phone and the one precious volunteer we had with us that day accepted my panicked request to supervise Carly. As if knowing the news was going to be difficult, I warned her we would be upstairs for several minutes.

Afterwards, Larry and I sat side-by-side on the couch and sobbed. I fell against him and literally began wailing. There was nothing we could say. We simply held hands and groaned, "Oh God.... Oh dear God!"

A thousand thoughts about past, present, and future swarmed the chaos of our hearts and minds. And many minutes passed. Finally I took a deep breath. Through swollen eyes, I looked into Larry's and asked, "What are you going to do? You're supposed to preach the sermon at church tonight!"

His topic...was Healing.

Pressing On, and God is Always Faithful

Despite the fact that our reality now had a mind-numbing name, God was keeping our hopes and expectations high. We were more convinced than ever that when God revealed miraculous developments in Carly, there would be no other way to explain them but a supernatural release of God's power and healing.

Angelman Syndrome, we had learned, is a rare genetic disorder. In eighty percent of cases, a specific region of the maternal side of the fifteenth chromosome is deleted. In other cases, that chromosome region is functioning abnormally. It is frequently misdiagnosed as autism or cerebral palsy with severe mental impairment. The prognosis includes:

- Happy demeanor
- Severe delays in all areas of development
- Lack of speech with severely limited use of signs and gestures
- Receptive communication skills higher than expressive ones
- Movement and balance disorders, usually with tremors and an

ataxic gait (moderate to severe difficulty coordinating a normal walking pattern)

- Hypermotoric behaviors (e.g., tremulousness, flailing movements), short attention span, and other behavioral uniquenesses resistant to therapies and behavior intervention strategies

Also common are seizures, sleep disturbances, feeding problems, obsessive behaviors, fascination with water, and microcephaly (significantly smaller than average head circumference).

Carly's genetic scenario was referred to as "deletion positive" which meant that a portion of the chromosome involved was missing. This suggested that she was among those most severely affected. It also at least partially explained her unusually challenging first couple of years. I say "partially" because her sensitivity to touch was remarkably profound even by Angelman Syndrome standards.

Having a diagnosis like Angelman Syndrome left very little room to explain away all of the developmental progress she was making as merely a result of "early intervention," "unusually committed parents," or even an "exceptional support system." These were phrases we heard often as professionals tried to rationalize the unexpected progress she was making. We were thankful beyond words for all of those things, most of all the people embracing hope with us. We were quickly discovering that our family's experience of a support system amidst life-altering diagnoses was far from typical. We did not take the loving attention for granted. In fact, for a long time, it quite literally carried us through. But, more importantly, we began to understand that God was going to use the devastating diagnosis to draw attention to Himself so that more people would know and love Him.

After Carly's diagnosis, some people asked us how it would change the program we were doing with her. The short answer was, "in no way at all." We were immediately concerned about the risk that people's expectations of Carly would change and be less helpful to her. We felt it was important to resist putting too much attention on a prognosis. No one could limit what God planned to do in her—no matter what any genetic code says!

By Thanksgiving, we had been busy with her program for eight months, six days a week. We were asked to give a testimony of our gratitude to God during the Thanksgiving Eve service at church. "You can have three minutes," they told Larry.

With so much to tell and so little time to tell it, using video was a natural idea for him given the training productions we were used to designing for our clients. Larry narrated while gorgeous images of Carly's progress came to the screen and demonstrated God's people working together in community to support her. The whole church owned the celebration that night and a spirit of overwhelming gratitude to God connected our hearts in a way that was palpable in the room. This was the script:

> *"...give thanks in all circumstances, for this is God's will for you in Christ Jesus."*
> 1 Thessalonians 5:1

The year 2000 has been an eventful year in Carly's life. While generally a time of happy progress and development, there were also some times that felt downright messy. Sometimes it felt like there were obstacles in the way or like we were rolling out of control. Other times it felt like our world had been turned upside down. There were even times we weren't quite sure how we'd gotten where we were, much less how to get out or where to go next. But the Lord has blessed us immensely and, I have to say, it's been a very interesting ride.

Nineteen months old as the new millennium began, Carly could not crawl and had very limited self-feeding skills. When we began Carly's program in March, she was just beginning to attempt a rudimentary army crawl on her belly. Today, after eight months of doing the program, Carly has made significant developmental leaps. She is cross-pattern crawling on her knees and elbows and she is much better able to feed herself and to drink from a sippy cup.

We are so excited and thankful for the progress she has made and we know that God has brought about much of that progress through the work and prayers of our volunteers.

Since starting the program, we have had over sixty volunteers come into our home. Some for an hour or two here and there, some for multiple hours every week. We want you to know that we thank God daily for the sacrifices you have made and continue to make for us. We deeply appreciate all your gifts of love, support, friendship, patience, kindness, generosity, wisdom, fellowship, and prayer. Especially prayer.

We know that there are many people who have been praying for Carly. Please know that your efforts do not go unnoticed and we pray that you will all continue to bathe her in prayer. We even have a neighbor who cooks a meal for us every Monday night.

So, as you can see, the Lord has wonderfully blessed us this year. We don't always understand why things happen the way they do. But we know that God loves us, He has a plan for all of this, and that He's walking beside us all the way. And I can see, especially at this time of Thanksgiving, that He's teaching us what true thankfulness really is.

"The King will answer them 'I tell you the truth. What you did for even the smallest of these people you did for me.'"
MATTHEW 25:40 (Worldwide English Version)

The sense of community that grew out of our crisis was a treasure we'll be hard-pressed to match in our lifetimes. We were increasingly energized to see how God was magnifying his handiwork. God was bringing a ripple effect of healing into other people's lives because of what was going on around Carly's situation, and even before that Judd's. God was creating a beautiful picture of how He designed community to work.

- One of our volunteers had suffered a stroke several months before stepping in to help with Carly. Lois had been more than skeptical about her ability to help due to weakness and incomplete tactile sensation on one side of her body. She started out as a timekeeper and stepped in when she could to help with the more physically demanding activities on Carly's program. Within a short period of time, she was excitedly telling us about the many ways God was healing and strengthening her body and reorganizing her tactile system because of what she was learning and trying herself at home. Later on, there would be even more to learn from Lois' discoveries!

- Other parents were empowered to explore therapeutic methods helpful to their children. Just as Judd had inspired us, so Carly was inspiring several others to embrace their potential. Amanda started driving a car and went on to college. Thea graduated out of special education. Nathan was crawling and using the computer.

- The gift of fellowship with volunteers, though often distracting us from the activities of Carly's exercises, were tremendously valuable. Volunteer enthusiasm was contagious and encouraging. One man frequently exhorted us to get enough rest and nurture our marriage. His words were especially convicting because he knew too well the loss of a severely handicapped child and the pain of a broken marriage.

- People reading "Carly Updates" would write back praising God for inspiration amidst their own trials. Our friends would even forward the messages on to other friends. Emails would arrive from people wanting to introduce themselves and share their thankfulness for how Carly had helped them see Jesus in their own situation.

- We would even encounter strangers who were praying for her. In a fast food restaurant one day, a woman heard us say Carly's name. Her eyebrows flew up and she said, "Is THIS the Carly my Bible Study small group has been praying for this past three years?"

Yet for all the ways that community had the capacity for blessing, it also had the capacity to distract us from depending on Christ alone for our strength and solace. So maybe it should be no surprise that just when God's light on that grand collective adventure was shining brightest, God chose that time to reveal the true nature of Carly's challenges and reinforce our need to stay completely surrendered unto Him.

God alone could heal the missing portion of Carly's fifteenth chromosome. God alone would give her a voice and words to communicate. God alone would heal her seizures and give her restful sleep. God alone would protect her from skeletal damage from delayed mobility and addictive behaviors. God alone would show us how to lead our family through what now was clearly going to be a very long and seemingly broken road. It was time to take faith, perseverance, and hope to a whole new level.

Nearly all of those volunteers remained with us for another three full years. During that time, we progressed through many milestones together:

- Carly started crawling on her forearms and knees regularly instead of rarely and sporadically…then a few weeks later started pulling herself up to stand at furniture.
- She started moving her tongue from side to side and then several months later would stick out her tongue momentarily after much coaxing with a sucker.
- Her vision improved so much, she no longer needed glasses.
- Bath time became a therapy session when we discovered she would stay up high on her hands and knees if only to keep her airway clear!
- She was responding to simple directions like "clap your hands," "stand up," "sit down," and "come here."
- Carly graduated from the cross-patterning portion of her program almost one year to the day from starting it. Within weeks of starting the next developmental activity (working toward walking), her posture was improving and her stamina for standing was markedly improved.

- Carly went from standing independently for three seconds in January 2000 to knee walking independently in June 2001. By November 2001, she was taking seven to twelve steps at a time without any support. She was three and a half years old. Shortly after she turned four years old, she was pushing herself up to standing and bear walking in the grass.
- She copied my words "kick, kick, kick" at a parent-child swimming lesson and was sometimes attempting to vocalize in response to questions.
- She learned to open drawers. Call me crazy, but we got excited about that! She was also starting to take the lids off of boxes to find hidden treasures (Cheerios) inside. Educators called that "object permanence." I called it "the family gene that will do almost anything for food."
- At four and a half, Carly was riding an adaptive tricycle.
- By five years old, she was using the bathroom successfully about once a day.
- Those little hands that pulled back in apparent pain years before would now hold the chains of a playground swing and reach out to give the warmest, most exciting hugs a person could ever hope to receive.

When Carly started Kindergarten, the "Carly Update" read:

Last Tuesday, Carly walked into Weaver Lake School with her sisters. To the rest of the world, it didn't seem like anything unusual but you will understand that it most certainly was! That was a week ago and I am still getting choked up just writing it down. It was an interesting day about which I can't adequately explain here. But one significant thing needs to be shared. It has to do with the overwhelming sense Larry and I had last week of the collective investment that has been poured into Carly that continues to bring her to milestones like the one she is now reaching.

We walked into the school as a family amid a surge of parents and children excited about their first big day back. And Carly walked too, holding one of our hands only to keep from being distracted. Larry and I looked at each other with knowing, tearful eyes, all-at-once recollecting the many perspectives we have heard about Carly's potential over the years. Some cautioned us that she would likely never crawl. Others warned that she would need some type of wheelchair at school because "even **if** she is walking by then" she most certainly wouldn't have the stamina to navigate long hallways. Others assured us that she would "plateau" in her development. And these kinds of perspectives might be understandable given that not all individuals with Angelman Syndrome walk, let alone with the quality and stability Carly does. In that moment of time, Larry and I admittedly felt a little lonely. We wanted to shout out to the masses of other parents proudly but so casually walking their children through the corridors, "DO YOU HAVE ANY IDEA WHAT A MIRACLE TODAY IS?!?!"

After we said our good-byes to Alex and Erin at each of their lockers, we stopped by Carly's room to show dad (who wasn't going to be able to come with me later that afternoon when it was time to drop Carly off for one of her two half-days a week in public school). As we greeted the special education teacher and a para, Carly indicated her need to use the bathroom then proceeded to go both ways on the toilet down the hall. So just in case Larry and I might miss the significance of the progress she has made, the Lord found another **huge** way to remind us what a remarkable scene we were witnessing. Yes, Carly had walked into Kindergarten and all the way around the school **independently** then **told** us she needed to use the bathroom and then did so **successfully**!

If there was any melancholy in that day for Larry and I, it was in longing for the chance to share that moment with all of you who have walked a long journey with us this far. After leaving Carly at school later that day, I came home and dropped to my knees absolutely overwhelmed by how many people have loved Carly and invested part of their lives and their faith in her. It is your hope that has helped us keep our own expectations and energy high, and it is your support that has been salve to our souls. We thank God for each of you with a gratitude that isn't easily expressed.

That enormous community of people surrounding us—volunteers, prayer warriors, friends, and family—also cried and prayed together through continuing challenges.

Seizures of all kinds came with intermittent frequency and varying degrees of intensity. Several lasted only a few minutes but others persisted for over an hour at a time. Carly endured seasons when drop seizures occurred hundreds of times a day. She would seize as often as every three to ten seconds all day long. That would go on for days and sometimes weeks at a time.

Sleep quality ebbed and flowed. The long, sleepless, and emotional nights far outnumbered the tolerable ones. We only slept more than a six hour stretch when we spent a night away from home a couple of times each year.

Constipation was another chronic and emotional issue on a daily basis. Digestive upset seemed to be at least one contributor to her destructive self-soothing behaviors.

Larry had recurring bouts with cellulites in his leg and was hospitalized twice. The lymphedema was managed but required tedious adjustments in his lifestyle and left him constantly vulnerable to dangerous infections.

We felt consumed by our life. Most of it seemed out of our control.

We were sick of feeling so self-absorbed yet the nature of our circumstances seemed to keep us stuck looking inward a majority of the time. On numerous occasions we both felt guilty about not serving more or even felt cheated out of opportunities to be involved helping with things we wanted to support in our community, at church, and in our daughters' school.

When we offered to simply pray for their activities, it felt like a cop out. It felt like we should do more. Then we would remember those people on our "Carly Update" distributions who told us they wished they could be more help. "I wish I could do more than just pray," they would say. Our reassurances to them would echo in our minds, speaking the truth back into our own hearts that prayer was the most important activity of all. We would remind ourselves that since everything good comes from the Father (James 1:17), no effort is worth pursuing without a covering of prayer acknowledging the authority, blessing, and power of Almighty God.

Sometimes staying in tune with God felt like a matter of survival. Other times, His presence was so unmistakable that we could only stand in awe of the Living God.

Like most people, we had often yearned for a more tangible sense of who God is and for the assurance that He is present and active in our lives. Each of us had prayed for this in various life circumstances. Now we were experiencing the reality of God's concern for the details. We were learning to see God's touch everywhere we turned. It grew to be kind of addicting. More and more we wanted to be alert to the presence of the Holy Spirit. Increasingly, we wanted to know God's perspective about life.

We had tasted and seen how good the Lord is. We wanted more!

Our Season for Finding Sanctuary

O God, you are my God,

earnestly I seek you;

My soul thirsts for you,

in a dry and weary land where there is no water.

I have seen you in the sanctuary

and beheld your power and your glory.

Because your love is better than life,

my lips will glorify you.

I will praise you as long as I live,

and in your name I will lift up my hands.

My soul will be satisfied as with the richest of foods;

with singing lips my mouth will praise you.

On my bed I remember you;

I think of you through the watches of the night.

Because you are my help,

I sing in the shadow of your wings.

Psalm 63:1-8

Chapter 5:
Stopping to Listen

One cold snowy day in January taught me (Lisa) a life-changing lesson about spending time quietly with Jesus. By God's grace, He was transforming my priorities and teaching me how to rest with Him. Had I not been learning to listen, we believe Carly would have died that day.

The sun was shining gloriously but everything was covered with a fresh blanket of deep snow that had fallen overnight, canceling school and Carly's program. As a result, I had three kids home, no volunteers to help, and Larry was away at work. Alex gulped her breakfast and suited up for a day of snow fort making. Erin, happier with a cup of hot chocolate than a sled full of cold snow, was begging to have a friend over. I started making plans to organize files in the attic immediately when Carly went down for her nap after lunch.

Despite having wound-up kids underfoot, I was excited. I love to get immersed in my To-Do lists or an organizing project so I had silently whispered prayers all morning that God would help Carly sleep for at least an hour in the afternoon. That would be long enough, I was sure, to make a dent in the chaos above the garage and satisfy my need to declutter.

As lunch neared, I felt pangs of guilt about having not yet taken time to sit with my Bible and spend even ten minutes praying and being still with the Lord. After lunch, Erin continued to talk about having a friend over and I was anxious to roll up my sleeves in the attic.

I put Carly in bed and noticed with excitement and gratitude that she seemed sleepier than usual. I shut her door and turned to head down the stairs for the garage. But as my hand touched the railing, my eyes caught sight of the Bible and journal laying in wait on my bed.

The tug of war began with a running conversation inside my head. "I should take just take fifteen minutes to sit down and do my Quiet Time. But I may not have much time up in the attic. Carly may not sleep long. Yes, but think of the satisfaction I'll have in getting my Quiet Time out of the way. But if I lay down on that bed right now, I'll end up falling asleep and then I won't get anything done at all! Maybe God knows I need a nap more than getting something tidied up. Maybe He cares enough about the fact that I really want to get that attic in order to excuse me from a time of Bible reading today. After all, it's been a day for unexpected schedule changes. I'm sure He has grace for me to spend just a little time doing something I really want to do. Yes, He does care about what I care about. But He wants me to spend a little time resting with Him **first**."

I sighed recognizing the truth in the chaos of my thoughts and yearnings. The most important thing I could do today was spend a few minutes with Jesus. And I knew from experience that He would honor my obedience. He would bless my sacrifice in some way.

Yet even as I sat down on my bed, I was having a hard time focusing. I reached for the radio thinking some praise songs would keep me from distracting thoughts as well as keep me awake. Something stopped me. I don't know what it was. I just had this sense that God kept insisting I learn to be really, really still. No radio. Just quiet. I sensed that I wasn't even supposed to open my Bible or start journaling right away. It was as if God was saying, "Lisa, I am not just one more thing to check off your list. I want you to relax with me and really enjoy being together. I want you to learn how to be still and just listen. You don't even have to rush to open your Bible or put a pen to your thoughts. Just wait with me silently in this moment."

And as I got sleepy sitting there on my comfy bed all quiet and cozy, I began to wonder if God was trying to woo me into a nap after all. But that wasn't possible anyway because the noise coming from Erin's room across the hall was distraction enough. Even as I lay there increasingly convinced that God must want me to take a quick nap, I was getting more and more frustrated with the noises coming from Erin's room that were now loud enough to risk waking Carly. "Perfect," I thought. "Now she's got a friend over and they're making noise in her room. They will wake Carly and I'll have lost everything. I won't have had a real Quiet Time and I won't have enjoyed my fun project either!"

So I started to storm out of my room towards Erin's bedroom door when I realized the noises I was hearing weren't coming from her room at all. They were coming from Carly's room.

As I opened her door, alarms were screaming inside of me. The noises I had been hearing were Carly gagging and choking. Frantically turning on the light, it was immediately obvious that her convulsing body was in a grand mal seizure. As I ran to pick her up, I hollered for Erin. I grabbed Carly in my arms and sat down in the rocking chair crying and praying, "No! No! No, Jesus! Please stop! Carly, please stop!"

"Erin!" I screamed at the top of my lungs! No answer.

I rocked Carly's rigid, pulsing body as my heart was breaking and tears streamed down my face. I had no idea how long she had already been this way but it must have been at least ten minutes. I screamed again several times until I scared myself at the tone in my voice.

Finally, a bewildered Erin appeared in the doorway. The quiet music playing in the background from her room quickly explained why she hadn't heard me and the sweet look on her face proved she was trying very hard to be considerate and helpful.

"Get me the phone and then go find Alex!" She stared back at me looking confused. "RIGHT NOW!" I begged and screamed barely with any breath left.

Calls to 911 and then Larry's office meant help was on it's way but when the police officer arrived several minutes later, Carly was still unconscious and in full convulsions. Another five long minutes passed and then the ambulance arrived. As I ran around the house throwing a bag of things together, the police officer told me Carly was vomiting. I grabbed some towels to put underneath her and then re-arranged her to make sure she remained safely on her side in a way that helped to prevent her from choking and aspirating. If Carly had been alone at this moment, still laying on her back in bed, it would likely have been the unrecoverable moment. In the meantime, the Emergency Medical Technician was preparing an injection to give to her.

It was a long, frightening trip in the ambulance. They insisted I ride in the passenger seat up front for safety so I turned and watched Carly's body jerking as I felt an overwhelming need to go hold her in my arms. Her body continued pulsing and lurching. I prayed they would drive faster or that the medication would do more to help her as I called my parents and Larry again on my cell phone. I opened the tiny Bible in my purse and hoped there would be something in one of the Psalms to give me hope and reassurance. But every time I looked back at Carly, her movements remained rhythmic, intense, and unchanged.

Another fifteen minutes went by. Then twenty minutes. And then twenty-five minutes into the trip to the hospital, we were finally there. The seizure had now been continuous for almost an hour and a half.

Larry met me outside the Emergency Room doorway and I collapsed into his arms.

After Carly was set up for an IV and given yet another type of medication, the intensity of her convulsions finally slowed. After another few minutes, the medical staff felt confident that Carly was now conscious but sleeping.

I had one hand on Carly, the other in Larry's. We leaned against each other and watched her sleep. Then I looked up into Larry's eyes and, with tears in my own, told him:

"God made me stop and listen today."

God's Voice Grew Clearer

Amidst all the activity and uncertainty that permeated those early days of Carly's life, one of the things I (Larry) most remember is how God impressed upon me the significance of stopping to listen. While some of this is attributable to the utter feeling of helplessness we so often faced, much of it had to do with the incredible resources God was placing around us to help open our eyes to His truth.

Listening is not something that comes naturally to me. Lisa just might attest to my distractible side. Stopping for anything other than a sporting event, the accumulation of information from the Internet, or a good nap seems pointless. And yet there we were, faced with tough decisions at every turn, sleep deprived and overwhelmed. We were at the end of ourselves. But God was there, revealing Himself to us in ways that I had not thought to pursue before.

For the first time in our married lives, Lisa and I were reading the Bible together and crying out to the Lord in prayer together. God had drawn us to a church that He used to really ignite my faith in Him. From the Sunday morning teaching, to the fellowship of those He surrounded us with, to the small group He had brought us into, God was speaking to us—to me. His ways seemed more real and tangible than they had ever been before. He wasn't just **turning** my ear to Him. He was, perhaps even more importantly, **tuning** my ear to Him. In John 10:27, Jesus says, *"My sheep listen to my voice; I know them, and they follow me."* I was beginning to know God's voice through His Word and prayer.

God also spoke to us through the counsel of wise, Godly people he placed around us. The Book of Proverbs told me of the importance these people could have in my life. Chapter 13, verse 4 promised, *"The teaching of the wise is a fountain of life, turning a man from the snares of death."* Verse 20 goes on to say, *"He who walks with the wise grows wise, but a companion of fools suffers harm."* Verse 15 of chapter 12 warned, *"The way of a fool seems right to him, but a wise man listens to advice."*

The Lord had blessed us tremendously with wise parents who prayerfully introduced us to the idea that a neurodevelopmental approach to Carly's therapy could have an incredible impact on her life. He placed before us wise mentors who exhorted us to present our needs to the church. He physically placed our home next to the home of a bold and wise woman who had great experience walking the medical road we now found ourselves on. And He imparted wisdom to us through various other friends and volunteers.

There is a wisdom that comes from age and experience in the ways of the world, and then there is a wisdom that comes from exposure to God's Word and a life lived in submission to Him. In almost every case, the people that surrounded us during this time had that Godly wisdom.

As we obeyed God one step at a time, He revealed more of Himself to us. We understood more about His character, more about His ways, and more about His love for us.

I'll admit it was challenging to be consistent. But as I spent time reading God's Word and praying, seeking counsel from others who were pursuing His wisdom, and trying to walk faithfully in God's will, I recognized a clarity in His voice that I hadn't experienced before.

Chapter 6:
Resting in "The Groove"

We know what it feels like to be bone tired. Nonetheless, it is our souls that crave rest even more than our bodies. Perhaps that is the real truth for all of us.

Some people crave food when they need comfort. Others depend on money and material things to make them feel confident or secure in stressful times. Here in Minnesota, many people head for a dock on a clear blue lake to watch a sunset in the summer or a deer stand to watch for a prize buck on a crisp morning with fresh snow in the fall. More than a few hunters call a Sunday morning in their deer stand "church."

Larry and I love water and docks and sunsets but we can live without the deer stand. Actually, Larry's usually good with a big bowl of popcorn. I mean a really **big** bowl of popcorn. I, on the other hand, like to soothe my inner restlessness with a good book, a gourmet meal, a nap in a hammock, a hot bath, organizing a closet, and de-cluttering my house —preferably all at the same time!

Humor aside, we have explored our fair share of opportunities to indulge our stress — mostly in healthy ways, but sometimes not so healthy. No doubt about it, we have craved plenty of things over the years.

We have craved sleep and relief from anxieties. We have wondered if there would ever be an end to Carly's hours-long bedtime routine and her middle-of-the-night wakings that set emotions flaring. And we have often been weary from the constant threat of seizures.

When Carly started school part-time, we had already seen six long years of very little sleep, a whole lot of therapy, and a virtually constant flow of people in and out of our home and life. Throughout her early elementary years, we continued her home-based program in the mornings with the help of a part-time caregiver. She attended public school for a couple of hours each afternoon. Though grateful for help, we found ourselves increasingly lamenting "can't live with 'em, can't live without 'em." It didn't matter how remarkable, even Divine, the support and friendship were from others. We downright resented being so dependent upon them. The whole situation felt like a prison sentence to a "fishbowl experience" of life.

So we have also craved privacy. We are grateful that we now receive some state and federal funding for people with disabilities. It provides essential respite and caregiver support for us. Yet we frequently feel vulnerable having people in our home. Our teenaged daughters don't always appreciate that dinner conversations, discipline, piano practice, and life are occurring under the watchful eyes of others. We can tend to feel judged or misunderstood. Our staff has always been gracious but there is no escaping the knowledge that there are always extra eyes and ears around. It is also wearing to keep "the team" trained, focused, and pumped up.

We have craved uninterrupted time with each other. We have resented the frequent interruptions to our own "bedtime routine." Believe us when we tell you, nothing ruins a moment like the crashing sounds of things falling off walls. Carly could suddenly decide that, rather than sleep, it would be more fun to kick her wall. We share that wall with her and it used to hold a shelf of books, a picture, and cute little bottles of essential oils. Those oils aren't so essential anymore.

Life is full of all kinds of hungers and thirsts. We have been tempted to seek comfort from many different places and have tried to pamper ourselves in some pretty creative ways. We have also been tempted to think, "if I could just get a few days of good sleep, or some time alone, or a romantic date with my spouse then everything would be fine." Sure, life would be greatly improved with any one of those things! But if we are honest, none of it is ever really enough.

The reality, we've learned, is that we tend to confuse our cravings for the stuff of life with our craving for a relationship with the Living God. Thankfully, God is tremendously creative and persistent in wooing us towards Himself. He has been drawing our hearts into a resting kind of relationship with Him. Being rooted in that relationship is like experiencing all the comforts of home yet it offers a kind of peacefulness that goes far beyond the weariness of our bodies and minds. It goes way down deep into our very souls.

We Are Satisfied by a Creative God

What we never expected was that our opportunities for extended quiet and nourishing times of prayer, reading our Bibles, resting, and being together would come in such creative packaging. One such opportunity presented itself as I (Lisa) sat in a hospital room with Larry. He was the one, not Carly, in the bed this time. It was his second hospitalization for cellulites in his leg and I was feeling guilty. Not guilty because he was sick again but guilty because I was enjoying it.

The troops had rallied to help at home so that I could spend most of each day at Larry's bedside. Even the tiny, stiff chairs and the crick in my neck weren't enough to cause me frustration. I was truly glad for the escape, the chance to be quiet and still with my husband. Honestly, I would open my Bible and thank God for using the frightening circumstance to give me a chance to run away. I would confess my selfishness and ask for Larry's protection and healing but go right back to loving every minute of it. We admitted together that we were feeling closer to each other and to Jesus in that place than we had in a long time.

Every resource available had been maximized to support our family, but no amount of help could provide the kind of strength or refreshment our souls needed for the long haul on such a life-changing journey. And we couldn't do life with Jesus in sound bytes.

If the first year on our journey with Carly was a season of being lost in chaos, and the next few were all about what God was doing to teach us about community, then this was the season when we recognized a desperate need to find sanctuary. We wanted to draw away to safe places of intimacy with God where we could trust him completely and find true rest.

We began praying specifically for an increased sense of what it could look like for us to experience satisfying solitude. And we asked those close to us to pray on our behalf. "Lord, open doors of opportunity for us to be with you — quietly, restfully, worshipfully — places where we can feel sheltered from life's challenges and nourished by You. Help us to be disciplined enough to embrace those opportunities when they come along. Show us how to create them — to **make** the time — too!"

We began to wonder if it is ever really possible to be prepared for what God will do, because in the years since those cravings stirred, God has surprised us. We have seen the creativity of an inherently creative God on a whole new level. God has unfolded for us a picture of how life can be lived more fully and more satisfyingly, even restfully, despite nearly constant challenges and overwhelming fatigue. We have discovered how to find sanctuary in our relationship with the Living God.

We are unapologetically passionate about our commitment to growing in our relationships with Jesus through prayer and Bible reading. We know it will always be our lifeline and the foundation we need to remain strong and fruitful. But knowing and doing are not always the same thing. Despite our best intentions, and even after the scare of a lifetime on that snowy day, our commitment has still ebbed and flowed. Life pulls our attention, energy, and affections in a myriad of directions away from the One True Source of comfort and rest.

It has helped us to remember the challenge we got from a small group leader who shook us into being consistent about our priorities.

The Challenge

I (Larry) vividly remember the night our dear friend Garth drew a line in the sand for all of us during a meeting of our

Bible Study small group. Everyone had been reporting poor commitment to personal time in the Word and intentional prayer. Those admissions had been going on for three or four weeks in a row when Garth asked everyone to throw their Bibles on the floor.

At first, everyone thought the challenge was rhetorical but he waited then repeated the request. He stood up out of his chair, stepped forward, and laid his own Bible down in the middle of the circle in front of us. One by one, each of us placed our Bibles with his and sat down expecting a bit of a lecture. What we got was a powerful and memorable challenge.

"Nobody, not one of you, is going to take your Bible back tonight if you don't really believe that what it says is absolute truth for your life and really be ready to commit your affections to God," he said. "This is serious," he persisted with growing passion. "What are we really here for if we're not going to hold each other accountable to doing our part in this relationship we say we want with the Lord God? Aren't we just a social group, some hope-to-help-each-other-feel-good club, unless we keep each other attentive to the Holy Spirit in our lives?" He paused and looked squarely at the Word of God on the floor.

"Don't take it back unless you really mean it!"

And so we all embraced our Bibles that night with renewed vision and mission. In some ways, we never held our Bibles in our hands in the same casual way again. There was a new reverence and a new sense of what our responsibility is to our fellow believers who desire to walk faithfully with God.

Jesus: Where "The Groove" Is

We have always found sailing to be a wonderfully relaxing activity. The warm breezes, spectacular scenery, and undulating waves make a heady combination. Finding "the groove" where the optimal angle of wind against sail sets our boat lunging forward with maximum velocity is an exhilarating experience. We have discovered that life with Jesus can be like that. We know because we are slowly figuring out how to do it. (We're not talking about nautical speed here, but we were feeling a bit of wind blowing through our hair!)

In the process of stopping and listening to the promptings and guidance of the Holy Spirit, we are finally learning to receive rest and refreshment in body and spirit. It is not the kind of comfort the world offers, though God surprises us with those kinds of gifts too. No, the kind of experience we are having, even during overwhelming challenges, involves a renewing and strengthening of our souls. In an exhilarating way, we are developing a sense of knowing God's definition of rest. It has brought to life that feeling of being "in the groove." Jesus said:

> *"Come to me, all you who are weary and heavy burdened, and I will give you rest. Take my yoke upon you and learn from me, for I am gentle and humble in heart, and you will find rest for your souls."*
> MATTHEW 11:28-29

Experiencing that kind of soul's rest means receiving faith that is strong enough to get us through, joy that endures even the sorrows, hope that withstands the fear of disappointment, and compassionate loving energy to step outside of ourselves.

Life on this side of heaven, we are discovering, is a process. And not a perfect one. Like constantly adjusting our sails for the changing winds, we need to stay continually attuned to the Holy Spirit. Just as our relationship with each other is growing and becoming more beautiful and enjoyable every day, so is our relationship with Jesus. Amidst the ups and downs of that process, we are making discoveries about how to live — not just living in the Light of God's saving grace, which guarantees an eternal inheritance, but a life here on earth that is full and exciting, hopeful and precious, enriching and joyful. A truly exhilarating life. Jesus also said:

> *"I have come that they may have life, and have it to the full."*
> JOHN 10:10

As we are growing in a lifestyle committed to resting in Jesus, we can genuinely shout praises to God that He is filling us with a peace that surpasses all human understanding. Our confidence and gratitude are increasing as we experience what it means to have the Lord God guarding our hearts and minds in Christ Jesus.

Living that way can also become infectious. Like any great adventure, our discoveries are practically begging to be shared! We want to take pictures. We want to show others how amazing the trip is becoming. In a strange way, we even want to go back and do it again because now we have more information and ideas about how to make the experience even better. We have a road map — a sailor would call it a navigational chart.

That is how the vision for a *Finding Glory in the Thorns* Bible Study first emerged. It's really how God's call on us as writers found its groove. We couldn't imagine that many people would be interested in reading a story about our journey through life-altering circumstances, but we could imagine ourselves sitting with small groups of others exploring together the discoveries we were making about living with faith, hope, joy, and purpose despite life's greatest challenges. With our Almighty Captain at the helm, we desperately wanted to see people gathering together in their thorny adventures and taking a journey to Glory!

So now we are about to dive in to the real deal. It's the part of the book where our story really starts intersecting with your story. It's the part where we all begin discovering how the pain and joys we experience fit into God's bigger picture — where we start sharing the vision for the eternal value of all this crazy stuff going on in our lives.

Get ready to set your sail. Put your heart up in the Wind. Let the power of the Holy Spirit keep filling you and filling you.

The journey has really only just begun — the adventure of a lifetime awaits!

PART 2

The Way to Glory

Lord, I don't know what to do with all
of this stuff that is out of my control.
I'm not sure I have what it will take to
make it through. Sometimes I'm very afraid.
I want to be hopeful about this situation
but I'm so often disappointed.
Sometimes I'm not sure I will ever truly be
happy again. There are times now when I feel
vulnerable around others yet I need so
much support. Is this as good as it gets?
I need to understand the meaning of this.
I find myself crying out like Moses did,
Show me your glory, Lord God!

Chapter 7:

Introducing the Road Map to Glory

We have discovered that many people who walk a road through suffering ask the same questions we have wrestled with on our journey:

How do I SURRENDER to God's solutions and timing?

How do I keep the kind of FAITH it will take to make it through this?

How do I hold on to HOPE when the risk of disappointment seems so real?

How do I experience JOY when this challenge is so consuming?

Is it worth SHARING my life with others, ugly parts and all, when asking for help and giving it are so hard?

Of course, waiting for the answers always seems to take way too long when we're in the midst of a struggle. But that is why God loves fellowship. It's why He loves church and small groups. It's even why He sometimes loves telephones, email, Google, and neighborly interruptions to getting the lawn mowed. When we bump into each other with our issues worn authentically and vulnerably on our sleeves, there is a good chance someone will resonate with our experience and learn something from it. There's a very good chance we'll learn something too. Thus, the opportunity is gained for an abbreviated time in the miry clay!

Won't you take a look at the Road Map that God has been showing us? Are you willing to stop and check for directions? If in any way you resonate with the questions we've had, this process will intrigue you. And God loves that because the same promises our Creator designed for us, he offers to you as well.

We have questions about SURRENDER...

Why is this happening and what should I do about it? Scripture insists that our salvation and satisfaction come only from a willingness to submit ourselves in faith to Christ. But how do we keep ourselves fully and consistently yielded to God's authority when there are so many specialists to see, so many strategies to explore, so many issues to manage, so much work to do in taking care of this situation, so many people's needs to balance, so many dreams unfulfilled, and time seems to be running out?

A peak at the Road Map promises this faithful direction: *Rest in the Faithfulness of God.*

When we frantically try to maintain control of our household, routine, and relationships, or desperately protect our comfort zones, when we hide our fears and yearning for validation, it is this challenge to surrender which re-captures our attention. The sovereignty and sufficiency of Almighty God is enough. More often, we remember to be on our knees first and trust the outcome to Him.

We have questions about FAITH...

How do we maintain the kind of faith that will get us through this — the kind of relationship with Jesus and understanding of God that will keep us strong, reassure us when we doubt, overcome our anger, and encourage us when we need comfort?

The Road Map reminds us to: *Saturate Your Mind with God's Truth.*

When we are grieving, battling depression, questioning God's plans or processes, or doubting his faithfulness and love, it is more important than ever to linger in God's Word. We are learning to be attentive to what God is saying and give **no** validation to the lies, accusations, confusion, or doubt planted by the enemy.

We have questions about HOPE…

Is it reasonable to hold onto hope? When the diagnosis, symptoms, labels, or related challenges don't seem to change, when progress seems insignificant or non-existent, should we keep hoping for a miracle? Should we keep expecting things will get better or at least easier? Or should we just accept that certain dreams are dead and that our lifestyle is changed (even doomed to struggle) forever? Is it our optimism or just disguised denial or are we rightly trusting God for a miracle?

The Road Map urges us to:

Anticipate the Surprises of God's Love.

When things seem hopeless, when prayers seem unanswered and God appears indifferent, we remember the various ways He has proven His holiness. He has awed us throughout Biblical history and He has surprised us in our own life experiences with unexpected treasures. With each passing year, we find it easier to trust the height, and depth, and breadth of God's unfathomable love for us. And we are praying for restored confidence that He will, again, do amazing things beyond what we could ever ask or imagine.

We have questions about JOY…

How do we experience joy within such frequent pain and sadness? Scripture indicates that we can and should rejoice in the Lord through all kind of circumstances making no exception for how difficult or easy those circumstances are. But how do we consistently have an experience of joy even during times of consuming fatigue, frustration, or grief?

The Road Map challenges us to:

Cultivate a Grateful Heart before God.

When we are caught in grumbling about our situation or stuck in periods of sorrow, we are learning to make time to worship God and practice gratitude. We recognize that it is ultimately

God who changes our hearts and gives us the chance to start over. He uses our obedience to His ways to transform our attitudes, emotions, and perspectives.

And we have questions about SHARING...

To what extent is this a journey we need to share with others or experience alone? Scripture insists that we share our stories and minister to one another. It doesn't let us off the hook when we're extra busy or because we are dealing with unusually challenging logistics in life. Neither does God promise there won't be pressure on our privacy, pride, or other vulnerabilities if we ask for help. So will He really make it worth it if we step outside of ourselves and reach out to others?

When we are struggling with issues of how to share what is going on, the Road Map promises we will:

Enjoy the Ripples of God's All-Consuming Comfort.

When we are tempted to withdraw from relationships, hide our challenges, or resist reaching out to serve others, we fondly reflect on how God has comforted and strengthened us through others throughout our journey. Yet more than that, we rejoice in the many ways that the intersection of our lives with others has enabled the release of God's transformational power. On this side of heaven, we now realize, we are seeing only a few of the ripples across the wide horizon of God's handiwork.

These answers to our questions are like the wind in our sails! When we face our deepest heartaches and greatest challenges to trust in the eternal perspective, we keep returning to this Road Map. As you read on, may it also lead you to the power and presence of the Living God where He fills those who trust Him with purpose and peace.

SURRENDER	FAITH	HOPE	JOY	SHARING
How do I **do** it?	How do I **keep** it?	How do I **hold** it?	How do I **experience** it?	Is it **worth** it?
REST IN THE FAITHFULNESS OF GOD	**SATURATE YOUR MIND WITH GOD'S TRUTH**	**ANTICIPATE THE SURPRISES OF GOD'S LOVE**	**CULTIVATE A GRATEFUL HEART BEFORE GOD**	**ENJOY THE RIPPLES OF GOD'S ALL-CONSUMING COMFORT**

SURRENDER

Then Jesus went with his disciples to a place called Gethsemane, and he said to them, "Sit here while I go over there and pray."
MATTHEW 26:36

FAITH

For though we live in the world, we do not wage war as the world does. The weapons we fight with are not the weapons of the world. On the contrary, they have divine power to demolish strongholds. We demolish arguments and every pretension that sets itself up against the knowledge of God, and we take captive every thought to make it obedient to Christ.
2 CORINTHIANS 10:3-5

HOPE

Now to him who is able to do immeasurably more than all we ask or imagine, according to his power that is at work within us, to him be the glory in the church and in Christ Jesus throughout all generations, for ever and ever! Amen.
EPHESIANS 3:20-21

JOY

Let the peace of Christ rule in your hearts, since as members of one body you were called to peace. And be thankful!

Let the word of Christ dwell in you richly as you teach and admonish one another with all wisdom, and as you sing psalms, hymns, and spiritual songs with gratitude in your hearts to God.

And whatever you do, whether in word or deed, do it all in the name of the Lord Jesus, giving thanks to God the Father through him.
COLOSSIANS 3:15-17

SHARING

Praise be to the God and Father of our Lord Jesus Christ, the Father of compassion and the God of all comfort, who comforts us in all our troubles, so that we can comfort those in any trouble with the comfort we ourselves have received from God. For just as the sufferings of Christ flow over into our lives, so also through Christ our comfort overflows.
2 CORINTHIANS 1:3-5

Chapter 8:
SURRENDER — *How do I do it?*

Have you ever come to a moment when you sensed that everything that was important about your life was coming to a crashing halt in that very instant? Some people call these "defining moments." But in some ways that phrase sounds almost too flowery or optimistic when the situation is a particularly unpleasant one. In any case, we've had a few moments like that and they have always been accompanied by a myriad of emotions — mostly fear, a little resentment, sometimes hope and anticipation, very often exhaustion, and well, mostly fear.

There was a day in January 2000 when we I faced one of those moments while reflecting on the devotions our friend Jeff led at our church's Annual Meeting. For several months we had been pondering and praying about a new therapy approach for Carly. She was twenty months old and significantly developmentally delayed. The approach we were learning about was based on non-traditional logic and methodology but made a lot of sense. It offered hope for developmental progress that we had been unable to achieve so far despite the prayers of many. We sensed that this resource was a tool God intended to use in helping Carly grow to her full potential, whatever that was.

This new approach would be incredibly demanding for our family. It would require us to ask others for a lot of help. It had the potential to move Carly along in her health and development in much more significant ways than what had been evidenced in over a year of the best and most frequent therapies our health insurance and school system could provide. At almost two years old, Carly was sleeping very little, unable to feed herself, barely rolling over, sitting up but quite unstable, not creeping or crawling, minimally interactive, and still crying much of the time.

The sacrifices we and others would have to make felt overwhelming and very uncomfortable. The realities of needing to depend on others for help made us feel exceedingly vulnerable. That's why, after first learning about the alternative neurodevelopmental strategies during the previous summer and fall, we had started implementing a small portion of them on our own. We knew that going to the next level was going to be life changing for us in many more ways. We even knew that some of these changes would be good and profitable for us and for Carly. But still we resisted. Even though we were encouraged by small but important signs of developmental progress from the new methods, we continued to drag our feet and pray that God would make it abundantly clear to us how He wanted us to proceed.

It was the first Annual Meeting Lisa had missed and to say she was frustrated would be an understatement. But caring for Carly was consuming. Taking her along wasn't an option since her frequent outbursts of crying were extremely disruptive. So I went alone promising to come back with a report on the business of the church. Instead, what I returned with was a vision and conviction that God had a Word specifically for us in Jeff's devotional from Joshua 3. Lisa saw the renewed light in my eyes as I explained to her what I had heard.

God was finally going to usher the Israelites into the Promised Land. It was a new day under Joshua's leadership. Though Moses had recently died and the people were likely wondering, "what's next?" the Lord was suggesting that the land of milk and honey was so near that all they had to do was cross the Jordan River. One problem. It was harvest time and the river was at flood stage. There were some overwhelming challenges. There were a **lot** of people including women and children to get over that river (apparently over two million in historical fact). And then there was that very heavy Ark of the Covenant to move over there too. But God had been speaking some great confidence into Joshua saying things like, *"Have I not commanded you? Be strong and courageous. Do not be terrified; do not be discouraged, for the Lord your God will be with you wherever you go."* (Joshua 1:9)

The Israelites were so convinced of the competence of Joshua's leadership that their attitude toward Joshua was *"wherever you send us we will go."* (Joshua 1:16) But there was still the little matter of that raging river. In Joshua 3:8, the Lord said to Joshua, *"Tell the priests who carry the Ark of the Covenant: 'When you reach the edge of the Jordan's waters, go and stand in the river.'"* *Later, as Joshua is describing to the people how this whole river-crossing expedition is going to unfold, he says confidently, "And as soon as the priests who carry the ark of the Lord — the Lord of all the earth — set foot in the Jordan, the water flowing downstream will be cut off and stand up in a heap."* (Joshua 3:13) And then, you guessed it, Scripture tells us that just as their feet touched the water's edge, the water from upstream stopped flowing and piled up in a heap so that the priests, the ark, and all of Israel passed across on dry ground. Amazing! It gave us chills just imagining the sight.

Although this story is very reminiscent of the Red Sea parting, we saw a fundamental difference. The first time God moved a great big bunch of water, the nation of Israel was fleeing an Egyptian army. They certainly must have been moving at a pace as fast as their feet and animals would carry them when Moses reached out his staff and the sea opened up before them so they could keep right on running away from what seemed like certain death. But, this second big water incident was very different. In this case, they were being required to take a very deliberate step of faith to which God was promising to respond with more abundant life than they had ever experienced before. They would be walking out into the Promised Land. But it was that very necessary step that came first this time. God didn't just open up the river so they could walk through it like He did with the sea. This time God waited. He waited to release His power and His promise until they had surrendered any fears or doubts and had taken that first step.

109

It's interesting that after those Israelites started walking, God did the critical work necessary for their freedom from captivity and abundant blessing. At this point in their journey, He required their faith demonstrated by the obedience of one single step.

But that did mean they had to surrender any expectations they might have developed out of previous experience. They couldn't just expect to have the Lord God open up a place for them to walk through while they stood patiently and passively waiting on the sidelines. No, this time, they had to have a different measure of courageous faith.

That is just so true about the circumstances of our lives! We begin raising a couple of children, for example, and we think we're starting to get the hang of things. Then he throws in a little twist. Okay, as in our case, not always such a little twist. Instead, He takes us to another level. Basically, he says "keep marching and I'll reveal myself along the way." Sometimes he requires us to be passive, to do nothing but pray and surrender all of it to Him. Other times He requires something of us. Not necessarily a lot, but some act of obedience that demonstrates our willingness to surrender to His will.

Sometimes that first step turns out to be the biggest one of all.

We determined that night that the "first step" for us at that point was in asking for help. We had gone as far as we could go on our own. God would not do more with us until we were willing to take this particular step. There have been many other first steps for us since then, but that first big step involved asking for help —making flyers and spreading the word in our church, in our neighborhood, through email, and in the community — explaining we needed the kind of help for our daughter that money couldn't buy.

We needed people who were willing to give us their time. We needed people who would spend an hour or so a week with us helping Carly with exercises and playful therapeutic activities that would give her a chance to grow. We also needed people to pray and pray hard — prayer warriors who were in it with us for the long haul. The whole situation would need bathing in prayer especially since we needed to maintain focus on the true Source of the blessings that we hoped and expected would come. With so much human effort going on, there was great risk that God might be forgotten and that man's efforts would be glorified. At that time, God's miracle was going to take the shape of a community of people making a commitment to share life with each other.

With this kind of vision, we had all the answer we needed. We'll admit, we're not sure it's the answer we wanted. But it was the answer we needed and God didn't take long to show us the reality of that! It is important to recognize that, with that vision, the Lord gave us the first real energy and focus we'd had since Carly was born. Remembering with new insight what God had done for Joshua and the Israelites helped us trust completely that it was going to be worth it for us. We were no longer debilitated by the fear of potential rejection. We no longer worried about being embarrassed if the unusual road we were taking looked foolish. We were ready to accept that having privacy in our home would be rare. We were no longer afraid that the intense nature of this venture would be dangerous to the balance of our family system. We had new confidence that God had our best interest in mind. We knew there would be challenges and even sacrifices but we didn't doubt that God would be there in the midst of them advocating for us and employing His perfect power on our behalf.

It was one of those kind of moments when you decide to take everything you've ever known about God to be completely true and trustworthy, and say to Him, "show me Your glory!" We were ready to lay it all on the line and let God be God. It was almost exhilarating! At least it was until I began to ponder what it would mean to open ourselves up to asking for help. I was not at all prepared for the level of surrender this would require. As our "designated family spokesperson," it would be my job to stand in front of our church Body — almost 600 people — and ask them to graciously volunteer their time in service to our family.

Surrender Confronts Fear

As I tried to organize my thoughts ahead of time, I often found myself identifying with Moses as he pleaded with God not to send him to free the Israelites from their captivity in Egypt. "What if I do a poor job of presenting our need," I thought, or "what if I say the wrong thing." As Moses said, *"I am slow of speech and tongue."* (Exodus 4:10) But it was not until I stood, shaking, before the congregation that day that I fully realized what my ultimate fear was: "What if they say, 'no'?" What if, after humbling myself by admitting that our family was in crisis and needed significant help, the people of the congregation decided to answer my request with indifference or, worse yet, outright rejection? I suddenly felt completely naked as I stood there.

The Lord was asking me to surrender any sense of control I might have over the situation. If this were going to get done, it would get done the Lord's way. And as the people in our congregation responded affirmatively to my request for help, I began to sense the promise of surrender, and our step into the Jordan was complete.

Our journey with Carly, with all three of our girls if we're honest, has brought us to some pivotal points like this when faith aligns with surrender. What grace God has for us when we are willing to hear what He has to say, trust Him enough to set aside that myriad of thoughts, emotions, agendas, and opinions we have on the matter, and simply obey Him. Unfortunately, we are often too stubborn to listen and submit until we've come to our "wits' end."

Whenever we have resisted those "wits' end" moments — stayed too busy, tried to shut our eyes to the truth, kept pressing on in our own strength hoping relief or success would come soon, been hesitant to let others know we are needing specific prayers — the painful grip of our circumstances squeezed even more life out of us than would have been necessary. Why are we so prone to hold on to what we can see when life has shown us over and over again that what matters is unseen, that God is sovereign and sufficient? Even as we write this, we are excited to remember how profoundly God has revealed His worthiness when we have been willing to take even one step of faith-filled obedience.

God Often Moves Us Out of Our Comfort Zones

Show us a place where you've become comfortable with your life and God just might show you a place He wants to move you away from. We all have our comfort zones — an easy chair in front of the television, a preferred nightly snack, hours of our favorite tunes on the ipod. And, most of the time, these attempts at finding comfort are normal reactions to stress. We escape to, even cling to what makes us comfortable when we are faced with uncomfortable circumstances.

This is not to say that God wants us to be uncomfortable all of the time. He wants only the very best for us. We are simply admitting that taking a look at where we feel comfortable with our lives has provided some clues about areas where God is challenging us to be open to something new. We have frequently discovered that around the corner to "something new" there has been a much greater fullness of life in store—fullness only available to a surrendered heart.

It's quite humbling and sometimes frustrating to think that God doesn't really need our help to accomplish developmental goals in Carly. He wants our cooperation with His plans because He takes pleasure in our fellowship and delights in our trusting partnership. God can do a miraculous work in her with or without us. Or not. We all know people who have worked really hard, tapped the best resources, or spent loads of money and reaped no good results whatsoever. We know others who have done no good thing at all yet they have seen a positive outcome.

According to James 4:3, our motives are a factor. It's one thing to engage in an effort out of an attempt to force God into making things turn out in a way that we are comfortable with. It's another thing to engage in an effort because we believe our activities align with God's process and then be willing to let the outcome be whatever God determines best. James 2:21-23 uses the example of Abraham's willingness to lay the life of his beloved son on the line and trust God's best for the outcome.

You see that (Abraham's) *faith and his actions were working together, and his faith was made complete by what he did.*
JAMES 2:22

Scripture is overflowing with examples of God challenging people to get out of their comfort zones. Mankind has a long history of resistance to God's challenges despite countless evidences that He is trustworthy. The Israelites wandered for forty years in the desert after failing to step out of their comfort zone when the Promised Land was within their grasp. Jonah avoided Nineveh because it was going to be uncomfortable and he paid a stinky price.

Thankfully, we have examples like the Apostle Paul to reassure us that following the Lord's leading is the option with the highest blessing. Paul's submission to the discomforts of persecution and imprisonment resulted in his authoring multiple letters that continue to testify God's life-saving messages for us more than 2000 years later. In the midst of these uncomfortable experiences and apparent obstacles, God was bringing life-changing knowledge and growth to followers!

We have seen this illustrated in our lives over and over again. One of the clearest examples occurred shortly after Carly started receiving school-sponsored therapy at home. As we have already described, Carly's early months were characterized by an extreme lack of sleep, very difficult feeding, and high sensitivity to touch and changes in temperature. From the moment we brought Carly home, we faced a constant cycle of feeding attempts followed by efforts to calm her enough so she would briefly fall asleep (twenty minutes at most) after which the cycle would start again. By the time Michelle, our first occupational therapist, arrived on the scene we were quite proud of the fact that we had achieved some level of quiet and routine. After nine long months, we could actually hold Carly in our arms to feed her rather than lay beside her holding the bottle.

One morning I was finishing up feeding Carly a bottle when Michelle arrived. As she observed our interactions with Carly, she quickly realized that our family was inadvertently establishing some obstacles to Carly's progress. "We have to get Carly out of her comfort zone," she calmly said.

I'll never forget those words. They pierced me like a knife. Tears flowed down my cheeks as I thought, "How could she say that after all we've gone through just to get to this point?" Our sole focus had been to get Carly into a comfort zone, and now we were being told that letting her stay there would prevent her from further development! It took us quite some time to digest that God was asking us to surrender our desire for comfort so that He could begin to bring additional healing into Carly's life. We needed to resist treating her like a china doll and continue parenting her. And, like so many other things, it is a process that continues to this day.

God shows us so much in His Word and, once again, Moses has been an inspiring model for us. Taking a closer look at Exodus 3:1 to 4:17 we see that God is showing compassion for the Israelites by rescuing them from the Egyptians and taking them into a *good and spacious land.* He is also modeling leadership that is surrendered and ultimately willing to be moved into a new manner of existence.

Moses is more than skeptical that he is the right man for the job of leading the people in their challenge of Pharaoh. Even when God reassures Moses that He will be with him, the questions continue: "What if this? What if that? Who am I?"

After many reassurances, the Lord gets personal with Moses. *What is that in your hand?* He asks Moses in chapter 4, verse 2. Imagine Moses looking at his hand and wondering what could possibly be significant to the discussion about what he is holding in his hand. A staff. A simple staff. But when the Lord God tells Moses to throw that staff on the ground, He is doing a lot more than getting ready to do a miracle. He is challenging one of Moses' comfort zones.

That staff represented much for Moses. It was used to guide and protect his sheep, also giving him a sense of authority and security in what he did for a living and who he was at that time. That staff was symbolic of Moses' livelihood and identity. It is likely that he did not often lay it down. Nothing in Scripture indicates it was particularly hard for Moses to lay the staff down. Chapter 4, verse 3 suggests he was quite prompt in obeying God's command to throw it on the ground. But Moses ran quickly away when God turned that staff into a snake! Yet even after several miracles designed to build Moses' confidence and equip him to effectively communicate God's message, Moses still resisted.

The Lord was, in the end, so gracious to Moses. He established the staff as a tool to demonstrate God's power, He gave Moses multiple reassurances that His help would be dependable at all times, and He offered the partnership of Moses' brother Aaron to further strengthen the team. But when it came right down to it, God expected Moses' trust and obedience. He wanted Moses to be surrendered to the Plan. And being willing to lay down that staff on a number of occasions was going to be a significant part of that Plan (v. 4:17).

We suspect that you, like our family and like Moses, tend to be tentative and argumentative with God when it comes to facing a really big challenge. We don't wish our weighty responsibilities on anyone else, but we sure wish God didn't seem to be dropping them in our lap either. Both of us have spent considerably long nights in Carly's bedroom crying out to the Lord, "Why can't she sleep? Why is she suffering? How long will you leave us in this situation? Why does it have to be this way? I can't take it anymore! What are we supposed to do?"

You have heard plenty about our sleep-challenged life already and, without a doubt, you'll hear more. For now, we humbly hope it challenges and inspires you to know that we always see progress when we are finally ready to admit our own powerlessness over the situation and claim God's authority over it. Many nights we have gone to bed praying: "Heavenly Father, we claim the power of Jesus' shed blood over Carly and our household tonight. Please grant each one of us sleep and safety. We know that you have the power to heal Carly completely with only a word from Your mouth. If it is your will, Lord, release that kind of power into her life tonight. If there is some greater purpose in your plan other than complete healing, please continue to equip this family with everything we need to remain strong. In your mercy, prevent Carly from seizures tonight and help her system to stay calm and find rest. Most of all, Lord, please give us Your peace."

Over the years, we've continued to discover many things we are inappropriately attached to. We regularly find ourselves challenged to consider what God is asking us to lay down before Him. The reality is that anything — yes, anything — which we hold onto too tightly may be considered an idol. And worshipping (idolizing) anything other than God is a sin.

Some of the stuff we have been challenged to lay down:
- The image that we had for our family and our future
- Lots of specific dreams (e.g., family vacations together, worshipping peacefully in church together as a family)
- The ambitions we had for our business
- Financial security
- Our ability to experience spontaneous, uninterrupted evenings as a couple
- Lisa's need for lots of solitude
- Any tendency to make Carly our "project" rather than God's own masterpiece in progress
- The desire to make people with "normal" lives understand
- Our love for cheese (Okay, so we had to give up dairy. Worse things could happen. Maybe.)

There are often patterns to be observed in Scripture and Moses' experience was similar to Joshua's at the Jordan River. God required one small act of faith, a willingness to step out of a comfort zone, and then He released His power. There are many New Testament accounts that continue in this same pattern. People reached out to touch the hem of Jesus' garments and they were healed, even forgiven! Sometimes the healing was only released after they first reached out in faith toward the Lord. God's work is amazing and wonderfully mysterious!

Life Comes After a Surrender to Death

In the life cycle, it is often true that something has to die before new and more abundant life can begin. It's God's design that things should work that way. Jesus prophesied the necessity and value of His own death in this way: *"I tell you the truth, unless a kernel of wheat falls to the ground and dies, it remains only a single seed. But if it dies, it produces many seeds"* (John 12:24). Yet, even knowing this truth, Jesus was sorrowful and troubled by the prospect of his death (Matthew 26:38). He knew what kind of pain He would endure and He begged God in prayer, *"My Father, if it is possible, may this cup be taken from me"* (Matthew 26:39a). Jesus was hoping for a way out of the pain and suffering.

Sound familiar? But that was Jesus' humanness. In His flesh, Jesus agonized for alternatives. Only because of the grace of Almighty God could Jesus find the strength to conclude His prayer this way, *"Yet not as I will, but as you will"* (Matthew 26:39b). Has it ever occurred to you that the very same grace and strength that was available to Jesus in the depth of His suffering is available to you in yours?

We take great comfort in knowing that even Jesus spoke honestly from His heart when He was anguished in his soul. Not once, but twice, Jesus made his plea (Mark 14:39). Yet he was ultimately willing to submit the end of the story to God's will not his own. And we all know now that the end of that story was the beginning of **life!**

Our former reality died the day Carly was born. In fact, our dreams (even a few we didn't even know we had) continued to die every time another diagnosis was added to her medical record or when another birthday would pass without the expected developmental milestones. And how resistant we still can be to submitting to the new reality! People are thrust into new, seemingly impossible realities every day. Children are born with disabilities, someone we love is diagnosed with cancer, and accidents tragically claim minds, mobility, and lives. Is it possible that we can be thankful that God allows a crisis to get our attention, to challenge our comfort zone, to shake us up, to form us into Christ-likeness if that's what it takes?

We will be the first to admit that we are not the same people, not even the same couple, that we were before Carly was born. To be sure, God has used each of our precious children to mold us and remake us. Our journey with Carly has unquestionably been a transformational one! We truly believe that the gift of Carly was the gentlest, kindest, most merciful way God could find to get through to us and fill our lives up with Himself. The new reality is that every time we are willing to let something of ourselves die, every time we are willing to lay down something we're holding too firmly, and every time we take a step of faith, God lets us taste and see His goodness. The beauty and fragrance and multitude of blessings He is revealing to us are part of our Promised Land and a window into what His glory means in our lives.

We simply don't have the whole picture. But God does. We don't know the end of our story. But God does. Will it have been worth it to stay within this daily, lifelong process of surrendering to God's will rather than desperately holding on to what we thought we wanted?

It most certainly will.

REST IN THE FAITHFULNESS OF GOD

*Then Jesus went with his disciples
to a place called Gethsemane, and he said to them,
"Sit here while I go over there and pray."*
MATTHEW 26:36

Practice these things while praying for God to increase your trust in Him:

- Take at least ten or fifteen minutes to stop everything and be completely still with God. Resist bringing anything into your time with the Lord except a Bible. Without music, candles, beautiful nature scenes, or any other "meditation helps" simply be quiet and still. (You might need to stand or sit on the edge of a straight-backed chair to keep yourself awake!)
- Read Scripture and let God show you His track record of faithfulness. Ask God to help you be reassured of His presence in your midst **today**.
- Make some lists. Write down your dreams, worries, fears, concerns, frustrations, and things you are needing to do (even those things you wish would get done but seem impossible). Where do you feel like you have lost control? What do you fear giving up? In what ways do you like life the way it is? In what ways might you be too comfortable with how your life is going?
- Tell Jesus what's on your mind knowing the Holy Spirit interprets the groaning of your heart to God.

121

- Listen. Are there words from Scripture hidden in your heart that God is using in this time to speak comfort or guidance or encouragement to you? Resist allowing your quiet times with Jesus to become a one-sided conversation. Allow God the opportunity to use Scripture and the promptings in your heart to show you His ways. A word of caution: If you sense a nudging toward anything that is inconsistent with Biblical guidelines, it is not a prompting from God.

Lord, You are worthy of my praise. I remember many times You have demonstrated Your perfect care for Your people from the beginning of time until now and I trust You to hold my life — with great care — safely in your hands. Help me hold loosely my comfort zones, dreams, plans, and goals so that if you call me to adjust or change them, I will be willing. Convict my spirit of any areas in my life that need to be more fully surrendered to Your ways. Reassure me that your ways are perfect and that I can always take complete refuge in You and trust the outcome to your perfect wisdom. AMEN

Chapter 9:
FAITH — *How do I keep it?*

The subject of faith takes on a whole new level of meaning when we are facing a crisis. When that crisis threatens our life, our quality of life, or the life of someone we love, we consider faith in the context of healing and strengthening. Will my faith bring healing? Do I have the kind of faith that it will take to get me through this?

We have desperately wanted healing for Carly. Through the tears she shed in the first hours after her birth, through her shrieks of pain that persisted throughout months of serious sores on her bottom, and through years of fighting for developmental milestones, we have prayed for her healing. We have prayed for a strength of faith that would withstand the waiting if God didn't respond quickly or in the way we expected. We have prayed for faithfulness that will prevail where doubts, worries, and fears creep in. Waiting in faith is a demanding part of living within the crisis of long-term, life-changing health or development issues.

There is Power in the Process of Waiting

Passages throughout Scripture promise that, if we have faith, God will heal. So when we pray and healing doesn't come, it's understandable that our faith might be a little shaken. Our natural tendency is to question God while we wait. Honestly asking God our heartfelt questions isn't necessarily a bad thing. However, in our process of waiting for the answers, the father of lies takes every opportunity to chip away at our confidence in God. It is helpful to remember that Jesus didn't promise a life filled with roses but He did promise victory.

In this world you will have trouble. But take heart! I have overcome the world.
JOHN 16:33

Lazarus' family had to wait three days for Jesus to come with His healing touch. And then even before Jesus arrived, it appeared to be too late! Lazarus was dead. Imagine the doubts that might have emerged during that three-day trek towards home. And imagine the family's disappointment when Jesus seemed unhurried. Now imagine how much more impact this event held in light of the fact that Jesus' power did more than heal, it brought Lazarus back to life! That's the nature of victory that overcomes the world! If only we could maintain confidence that when Jesus seems unhurried, there is something even more powerful to reveal on the other side of our journey. Unfortunately, the enemy uses doubts, fears, and worries to attack that confidence.

Some of our most pervasive doubts have to do with whether Carly will ever reach certain levels of independence. We wonder whether she'll play meaningfully by herself without near constant one-on-one facilitation. Will she walk with enough dependable balance to be completely free of arms-length supervision? Will she ever speak to us with clear words or use body language to express anything more than her most basic needs? Miraculously, at nine years old, Carly has already exceeded many of the expectations specialists had for her whole lifetime. She has even spontaneously said the words "I love you" on a number of occasions. This should leave no doubt that God can do seemingly impossible things. Yet despite all of that, we continue to live with doubts about her potential.

We worry that she'll die of a seizure. We get anxious about the possibility that she will be injured in a serious fall. We are gripped with fear when we consider that she could wander away from us into danger. We wonder if she'll end up institutionalized some day because we are physically unable to care for her anymore. None of these thoughts are helpful. The enemy is unseen but ever present in trying to shipwreck our faith. Thankfully, God can use for good what Satan intends for bad but allowing ourselves to linger in these kinds of thoughts serves only to give them a foothold. We do well to stay on guard, keep our radar up, and fix our course on what we know the Bible says to be true. The enemy is not trustworthy. God is eternally trustworthy.

Throughout our journey, we have seldom known what was coming ahead of us. For that, we are largely thankful because if we'd known what challenges and obstacles were lingering in the future, we would have had a lot more to worry about!

We have learned from our sailing adventures to steer clear of obstacles like other watercraft, unexpected rock outcrops, or adverse weather conditions. The common denominator of all of these obstacles is that they can be seen. But there is one obstacle in sailing that cannot be seen with the naked eye: the bottom. A depth meter can tell us how deep the water is directly underneath us. But what about the depth immediately in front of the boat? What if the boat drifts a little and we are unaware? Charts give us a general idea of depths in the area, but they are not designed to be detailed topographical representations of the lake bottom.

Despite the tools that are available, we still can't see what is coming toward us under the water. God has always known what was ahead for us. He is perfectly trustworthy as our Supreme Navigator as He fights a largely invisible battle with very powerful weapons.

> *For though we live in the world, we do not wage war as the world does. The weapons we fight with are not the weapons of the world. On the contrary, they have divine power to demolish strongholds. We demolish arguments and every pretension that sets itself up against the knowledge of God, and we take captive every thought and make it obedient to Christ.*
> 2 CORINTHIANS 10:3-5

When sailing, we also need a certain water depth in order to operate safely. The keel of our friends' boat reaches almost seven feet under the water. We got nervous any time we had less than twelve feet below us. With large swells added to the equation we needed significantly more depth. We've had experiences of either running aground or coming extremely close. While we've been spared significant damage, it is not an enjoyable experience to be uncertain about what's coming in front of us.

One of the most significant ways God gives us depth and maturity in faith is by saturating our mind with the truths of His Word.

> *For the word of God is living and active. Sharper than any double-edged sword, it penetrates even to dividing soul and spirit, joints and marrow; it judges the thoughts and attitudes of the heart.*
> HEBREWS 4:12

God's Word brings our thoughts, negative attitudes, and troubled emotions back into safe waters. Power comes to our process of waiting for healing when we take up the Lord's weapons. At times, Larry and I have grown resentful and covetous. Sometimes we have to bite our tongues when other parents talk about having to get up at night to nurse a baby, change a diaper, or care for a child who has been sick for a few days. Whether the issue is sleep, finances, or seemingly less complicated lives, there can be much to feel jealous about. So there is tremendous faith-building power in reading something from Scripture that resonates with a timely and deeply personal message. For example, just as we were recognizing a bitterness rising within us towards those whose lives seemed simpler, this passage rose up off of the pages.

> *But as for me, I came so close to the edge of the cliff! My feet were slipping, and I was almost gone. For I envied the proud when I saw them prosper despite their wickedness. They seem to live such a painless life; their bodies are so healthy and strong. They aren't troubled like other people or plagued with problems like everyone else. Then I realized how bitter I had become,*

how pained I had been by all I had seen. I was so foolish and ignorant—I must have seemed like a senseless animal to you. Yet I still belong to you; you are holding my right hand. You will keep on guiding me with your counsel, leading me to a glorious destiny. My health may fail, and my spirit may grow weak, but God remains the strength of my heart; he is mine forever.
PSALM 73:2-5, 21-26

During another faith-testing night, Lisa came stomping back to our bedroom crying and jolted me out of sleep with some abrupt statement like "I can't take it anymore!" There was nothing to say. All I could do was lay there holding her. We remained like that together for more than an hour and went to church the next morning feeling totally drained. The sermon covered Psalm 46. The theme: Be Still & Know that He is God. A few days later, Lisa received a card in the mail from a friend at our former church. Having no idea about the particular week we'd had, her note simply reassured us that she was praying and understood the weight of our challenges. The verse printed on the card was *"Be still"* from Psalm 46.

Whether we are tired or not, there are many vulnerable times and places the enemy finds to wage his attacks. Making a point of exposing ourselves to the words of Scripture gives God opportunities to stay out ahead of us with faith-strengthening truth and encouragement.

We Have a Trusted Navigator

Those of us living within the context of life-altering circumstances know that there is hardly an end to the list of potential resources and perspectives available. Surely if we look hard enough, long enough, and effectively enough, we will find the answers. But does God require us to work so hard? Or does He simply require faith?

A couple of years ago, we were in a Bible Study with a friend who posed a challenging question to our small group. "I think

God helps those who help themselves. I have a lot of trouble with the whole idea that we are just supposed to sit back and do nothing—you know, just trust God on faith alone. Do you really believe God expects us to do that?" he asked. It's a legitimate question. If we picked ourselves up off the couch long enough to research the options and then focused ourselves on working hard, wouldn't God honor our efforts and work out success for us? Scriptures could support both approaches. Jesus healed people based solely on their faith. Yet there were also times when the hurting had to reach out for healing. Even if only to touch Jesus' garment, some initiative and effort were involved. Our challenge with praying for Carly's healing was in determining which resources to use while trusting, in faith, that God would release His power through them.

There are so many strategies and methods to consider, and so many opinions from medical professionals, educators, family, and friends. There are countless medications, diets, standard and not-so-standard treatments, tests and diagnostics, and alternative therapies to explore. The research process and endless Internet links can be overwhelming. How can we ever know that we are following the right protocol and not missing some critical information? How do we know which alternatives are legitimate and which ones are not worth pursuing? How do we know if we are supposed to just sit back and trust God or work hard engaging certain strategies or efforts of our own?

If we don't have the Almighty Navigator guiding us, then we can't be sure of anything. Many wise, enthusiastic, and well-intentioned people have over-stepped God and believed they have found the better treatment strategy, the better specialists, or the better hospital. We need to pray for wisdom and discernment, for open and shut doors, and that God will make our paths straight. We need to resist being driven by our fears, our need to be in control, or even our love for someone. None of those things justify racing ahead of God. We must be driven solely by the Spirit of the Living God who stands in ultimate authority over any progress made. Larry and I have grown very anxious over the years whenever Carly's developmental progress seemed to stall out. In our pride, we have passionately embraced rebellious attitudes towards those who claim Carly's development will plateau. While we may be justified in disagreeing with perspectives that limit her potential, that has never justified our running ahead of God when we thought we had a perfectly good idea about how to proceed.

We have utilized a variety of non-traditional resources to help Carly. Because most alternative methods are not widely publicized, it has been challenging to both locate those resources and to discern which ones may be credible options for us. When science, professionals, even family and friends are skeptical, it is particularly hard to know if we are just grasping at straws or following the true leading of the Holy Spirit.

Did Joshua struggle with skeptics when God insisted He lead the people in a battle using very non-traditional methods? In Joshua chapter 6, the Lord describes a remarkable plan to Joshua. God was giving Jericho to the Israelites and his plan involved crumbling the walls around the city after having the Israelites march and blow horns for seven days. Israel was ready to attack but the Lord had an alternative approach in mind. While on the surface it seemed like an unusual plan, nothing in God's Word indicates that there was any hesitation. The priests and God's people assembled immediately to take action on Joshua's instructions from the Lord.

Another thing impresses us about this battle at Jericho. The Israelites didn't get carried away in zealous faith by rushing ahead of God's plan. Those Israelites displayed a radical trust in God to have obeyed Him even when the plan required great patience and must have made no sense to them at all. It is arguable whether the Israelites had adequate resources to launch a traditional attack successfully. With God on the Israelites side and quite a reputation preceding them—parting seas, clouds of fire, stopped up flood waters—even the citizens of Jericho feared the Israelites would be victorious.

So it might have been understandable if the Israelites had said ever so humbly, "Lord God, you have supplied for all our needs for more than two score years now. We're ready to move on and we know we can trust you to give us this victory. So how about we don't waste any more of anybody's time? We are ready to press on with the strength you've built up in us with that nourishing manna stuff. Honestly, we see no need to dally around and wait even a few more days.

"Yet day in and day out, for a whole week, they marched quietly around and around that city. Not one of them succumbed to an urge to re-assemble the troops and charge in for battle. But by the end of their seven-day parade when the walls of Jericho collapsed at the shout of their voices, you can bet they charged straight into that city and captured it"
JOSHUA 6:2.

God's ways don't always make sense to us. The resources He sends our way can come in unusual packages. We simply cannot limit what He might do by praying only for the things we can imagine that He would do. God is able to do *"immeasurably more than all we ask or imagine"* (Ephesians 3:20). God forbid that we should expect Him to do anything less than something entirely amazing! Joshua is an extraordinary model of faith lived out in obedience to God. As a result of his God-focused leadership, the Israelites witnessed miraculous victories in the face of impossible odds and incredible things were done on their behalf. Oh, that we could have that kind of courage. Oh, that we could have that kind of trust that listens to God when He suggests unusual things. Oh, that we would be so obedient!

We have tried to be attentive to the strategies we believe God has Divinely appointed for us with Carly. We have prayed long hours to understand when the Lord was prompting us to pursue certain resources or when He was simply telling us to wait for Him to be more clear.

It has been tempting for us to get caught up in researching medical information or treatment options on the Internet. The amount of information available is both empowering and overwhelming. It is easy to run ahead of God or to become debilitated in confusion by all of the alternatives. We have found it tremendously helpful to be in active prayer whenever we start digging around for answers or trying to make decisions. We have often prayed this way: "Lord Jesus, I need your help right now in sifting through all of the information available to us. I don't believe you want us to take any more time than necessary away from the other things you want us to do today and the people you want us to be with. So direct my eyes and my mind to what you want me to find here. A lot of what I can find is valuable information but not all of it is useful to us. So bring the critical stuff to the front quickly, Lord God. Impress on us what is wise and helpful so that we can move forward without distraction and according to Your will. Help me to know when to stop and move on so I don't waste the time given to me."

When God has led us towards effective resources we have sometimes become vulnerable to pride. When issues like seizures, sleep, blood pressure, cholesterol, weight, and lymphedema have been out of our control, God has gently shown us when we are not seeking Him first. He began making this lesson clear as we were learning about nutrition and the role it could play in healing our family.

Alongside our dearest friends, we have spent several years studying health management strategies according to traditional Biblical principles. Exploring God's design for health is exciting and empowering. We have grown increasingly enthusiastic about how a nutritional lifestyle can have a significant positive impact on the health of our families.

It's a great blessing to share similar perspectives and goals with close friends. It certainly makes it easier to coach our children about making good eating choices when they find the same weird and stupid stuff on the pantry shelf at their friends' houses! As we gain knowledge and experience, we pray together for wise, disciplined children and healthy families. But more importantly, we also hold one another accountable when our focus gets off kilter, when we are tending to depend on our own understanding rather than leaning on God.

Nonetheless, there have been many times one of us has gone to our cupboard of supplements and homeopathic remedies or even to the doctor for an antibiotic before **first** remembering to lay hands on our sick child or Larry's red, hot, infected leg in prayer. Like many families facing serious or chronic health conditions, the list of specialists we've seen is long. We have read many books over the years, sought counsel from numerous medical and educational experts, and brainstormed with godly friends and family. The book of Proverbs affirms that, *"The heart of the discerning acquires knowledge; the ears of the wise seek it out"* (18:15).

But there is an important distinction between seeking out wise, godly counsel and actually elevating its importance and allowing prayer to become the last resort. Everything is possible only when we surrender our course to the Almighty Navigator in faith!

In addition, and much to our dismay, we simply cannot do everything that would be helpful for Carly. Even if all of the necessary resources were available, we would need enough money to buy them, enough energy to implement them, and the best knowledge and skills to conduct them with quality. Furthermore, there are five people in this family that have various important needs and those must be kept in balance. We are inadequate to meet each person's needs perfectly because when God created us, he didn't give us an unlimited supply of time or energy.

How humbling it is to admit that if we could perfectly meet each other's needs we would not need God. Even if we were able to identify every strategy that would be fruitful, if we found just the right medication and determined the most effective dose, if we followed a perfect diet, if we completed one hundred percent of Carly's therapy program every day, there would always be even more that could be done.

God has given us a rich supply of resources to accomplish the plans He has for Carly's life but we also recognize His wisdom in limiting our capacity to accomplish perfect implementation because where our resources end, His power is most evident and our faith can take wing! We will always fall short of perfectly implementing the plan. We are human after all. Only God can be God. Thanks be to God, we can trust in the same promise that God made to Paul:

> *But he said to me, "My grace is sufficient for you, for my power is made perfect in weakness."*
> 2 CORINTHIANS 12:9

When Jesus fed more than five thousand people on five loaves of bread and two fish, that small amount of food was enough for him. God can use what relatively little we have in terms of money, time, energy, wisdom, support and make it sufficient. With every day that passes, every crisis that comes and goes, we appreciate that no amount of wisdom, skill, or resource is good enough if it isn't, before everything else, surrendered in prayer to the authority and plans of Almighty God. It is a constant struggle to be on guard about where we are placing our faith. It's one thing to say we are trusting and depending primarily on God, and it is another thing to fully live in that reality.

So often when we encounter a crisis, we throw ourselves for days or weeks into all the treatments anyone can recommend or accomplish. And then when there is no progress, we finally put out a call to our prayer warriors on the 'Carly Update' list. Sometimes within hours of our posting to them, the tides change. It is no coincidence that the issue finally resolves or moves into a significant stage of relief at that point. The Lord waits for us to surrender to His authority in faith and ask for help.

Our own knowledge and resources will never be enough by themselves. Yet when touched by the power of God, they become sufficient. When we seek the counsel and power of the Almighty Navigator, then all we have is enough.

What Really Matters to God?
One of the big theological questions we have faced in life with Carly has to do with healing. Would the Lord heal her? If so, would it be a quick, miraculous healing, or more of a long-term process?

Lisa and I believe completely that the Lord has the ability to heal Carly in an instant. But we have felt throughout this journey that her healing would unfold gradually over the course of some time. We have sensed and seen that the Lord has much He wants to accomplish through her life and therapy program. The stories of many of our volunteers testify to it. Many have either experienced healing personally through working with Carly or have been connected to resources that have led to healing in other family members. Their own stories of healing journeys bear partial witness to all that the Lord is accomplishing in and through her life. God seems to be getting a lot more mileage out of making her healing a process.

To a large extent for us, prayer for Carly's healing has become a selfish prayer. Certainly our lives would be easier if she were like a typical child! But God might not get the maximum benefit for his kingdom in handling it that way. That is not to say our ease, comfort, and concerns don't matter to him. It's just that He has a Divine perspective on what is best for us and all of those others around us.

Ephesians 3:19 explains that the depths of God's love surpass our ability to comprehend. Because of this truth, it makes sense that the expression of His love for us might sometimes be confusing. It is entirely plausible that God's best lies right in the middle of this thorny life we're living.

When we started writing this book, we asked Alex and Erin what some of the most important lessons are that they have learned on their journey with Carly as their sister. Erin's immediate response was an exciting testimony of the faith God is developing in her. "Well, I know now that God will **always** answer your prayers!" she wrote. "Sometimes he says 'no,' and sometimes he says 'yes,' and **sometimes** he says 'wait.' In our case, that was what he said! He said we had to be patient and wait so that He could take the time to work with Carly, and He did exactly what he said He would do! He has helped Carly to grow and learn! No plateaus here. Slowly but surely He is answering those prayers!"

Over the years, we have had many discussions with other believers about the subject of healing. Most of those discussions have supported our belief that Carly's healing would be a process. Others have been more difficult conversations to have, raising questions about the state of our faith ("if Carly is not being healed it must be because your faith is not great enough") or intimating that some sin had caused Carly to have seizures or to be born with Angelman Syndrome in the first place. Sometimes health issues are the consequence of sin. Often, they are not.

A pastor offered the comfort that, once in heaven, Carly would be made perfect. But how much do we really understand about God's idea of perfection anyway? Scripture says that each of us is fearfully and wonderfully made (Psalm 139:14) and already a masterpiece.

"For we are God's workmanship, created in Christ Jesus to do good works, which God prepared in advance for us to do"
EPHESIANS 2:10

God has already gone out ahead of Carly preparing ministry for her to do. All who have witnessed Carly's life so far agree that she has ministered to countless people on transformational levels that the rest of us hope for our lifetime!

One of the most important lessons I (Larry) have ever learned about healing was taught to me one summer night in 2004. We were at an early evening soccer game that our oldest daughter Alex was playing in. The weather was very warm, and Carly had difficulty regulating her own body temperature. Getting overheated also triggered seizures. So while Alex, Erin, Lisa and I proceeded to the game, we left Carly and her caregiver, Jenny, in our air-conditioned van in the parking lot where they could stay cool. Erin went with me over to the spectator side of the field while Lisa, serving as an assistant coach, and Alex went to the other side of the field to take their places with the home team.

As I arrived at the game, I was still mulling some things that had happened at work that day and my frame of mind was not positive. Erin was playing with a sibling of one of Alex's teammates. She came to me to show me the toy she had recently gotten, now broken. She explained that a little boy with one of the families of the opposing team had taken the toy from them and, as he was playing with it, broke it. My internal temperature rose another degree or two.

As the first half of the soccer game went on, Alex's team was not playing particularly well. The July heat and humidity made it additionally uncomfortable. And to top it all off, the same boy who had broken Erin's toy was now jumping up and down on the aluminum bleachers just behind where I was sitting, causing a very loud, repetitive, headache-inducing sound!

As halftime arrived, the score was 2-0 in favor of the visiting team. The cumulative effect of all of these events had taken their toll on me. It was now official—I was in a full-blown **bad mood**!

I looked over toward our van in the parking lot and saw the door swing open. Out climbed Carly with Jenny's assistance. As I watched them walk hand-in-hand across the open soccer field, my mind raced back to the many times when we wondered if she would ever creep or crawl, let alone walk. As Carly got close enough to see me sitting along the sideline in my folding chair, her face lit up with a bright smile and she cast aside Jenny's hand to set off in my direction by herself.

As she approached me her excitement grew, as did her grin. She climbed up on my lap, reached up to give me a hug and a kiss, and then laid out fully on my lap while pulling the bottom of her shirt up just above her belly button—Carly's universal sign for "tickle me!" And that is what we did! We played tickle and wrestled and hugged, all while Carly's laughter rang out on the sidelines.

As the teams began to take the field for the second half, I looked down at Carly, smiling and laughing, and I began to realize that my mood had completely changed. Feelings of anger, resentment, and irritation were now replaced by contentment, joy, and love. At that moment, the tears began to stream down my face. I thought to myself, "Who needs the healing?" I imagined the Lord looking down upon Carly from heaven and saying, "Well done, good and faithful servant!" And then I imagined the Lord looking down upon me, a sin-filled creature prone to anger and bad mood. He was saying, "My grace is sufficient for you, for my power is made perfect in weakness."

Could it be that we are not looking at faith and healing from God's perspective? Could it be that, instead of focusing our priorities on the potential for strong health and development, we should be focusing on our spiritual potential to become more like Christ? The need for healing is at least as much a spiritual one for most of us as it is a physical one. God is most urgently interested in what's going on inside of our hearts. He is constantly seeking more intimate connections with us. He will use every opportunity and every individual, regardless of the condition of their health or the stage of their development to draw us more closely to Him.

It matters to God that we lean not on our own understanding but saturate our mind with His truth.

Let us keep our eyes fixed on Jesus, the author and perfector of our faith, who for the joy set before him endured the cross, scorning its shame, and sat down at the right hand of the throne of God. Consider him who endured such opposition from sinful men, so that you will not grow weary and lose heart.
HEBREWS 12:2-3

SATURATE YOUR MIND WITH GOD'S TRUTH

For though we live in the world, we do not wage war as the world does. The weapons we fight with are not the weapons of the world. On the contrary, they have divine power to demolish strongholds. We demolish arguments and every pretension that sets itself up against the knowledge of God, and we take captive every thought and make it obedient to Christ.
2 CORINTHIANS 10:3-5

Practice these things while praying for God to increase your Faith:
- Each day for the next week or two, read about one of Jesus' miracles in the Gospel of John. Skim the book and select those that seem interesting to you. Pause and think about how each sick or hurting person felt. Consider how Jesus responded and why He handled each person the way He did. Re-read the passage and pray that God will continue teaching you more about His heart.
- Think about the issues you are struggling with and consider how Jesus would respond in light of what you are learning about Him.
- Write down any verse(s) that stands out to you, especially any that emphasizes the truth of what God desires for your situation. Use a journal and/or index cards or self-sticking notes of paper. Post those meaningful verses in a place where

you can reflect on them at least twice every day (e.g., on the bathroom mirror, near the kitchen sink, at your desk, on the dashboard of your car, in the shower).
• Consider memorizing any verse(s) that holds special meaning and inspiration for you.

Thank you, Holy Spirit for the power You have to heal people, body and soul. Show me how to wait patiently, faithfully, and expectantly for a release of your power. Help me to recognize the thoughts, feelings, and doubts I hold deep within my mind and heart. Thank you for understanding all of them, even if what I think and feel isn't always positive. Thank you for the power of your Spirit in me that enables me to live free from bondage to lies. I want to surrender any mindsets I have that are not helpful and ask that you renew my faith by your mercy and grace today. I want to live in faith, believing the true promises of Scripture that your love for me will never fail. AMEN.

Chapter 10:
HOPE — How do I hold it?

Several years ago our friend Bruce shared with us how he had been praying for his young son every night when he tucked him in. Nathan has cerebral palsy. He is an absolutely brilliant boy with a contagious smile, amazing sense of humor, and wisdom beyond his years. He is a boy who is developing a beautiful godly character and love for Jesus but who has very limited mobility and verbal skills. So understandably Nathan's parents had much to pray about on his behalf.

A few years ago, Bruce candidly shared with us about a struggle he was having. It was a common struggle parents of children with disabilities have but one often held in secret silence. So we were glad Bruce was willing to be vulnerable and share his heart with us because we resonated with it, felt less alone, and grew more inspired to join him in discovering God's heart in our situations.

Bruce explained that he had started out praying regularly and with boldness for Nathan's healing. He and his wife Barb had great faith that God could do the impossible in their son's life. They firmly believed that they could wake up one morning and find Nathan completely well. Their hopes were very high. They knew God had the power and authority to do that. They respected the perspective that sometimes healing comes through a process but didn't believe that was the way God was planning to work out a miracle in their son.

So after a while when the healing didn't come Bruce grew weary and even angry with God. He admitted it had simply become too disappointing to hold on to hope. He couldn't bear to lay his heart on the line like that every night and face an unchanged reality in the morning. He quit hoping. For a while, he admitted, he even quit praying about it at all.

We had similar experiences during many long nights of Carly's sleeplessness and behavior challenges. We regularly felt hopeless, angry, abandoned, and confused. The first time we ever remember Carly sleeping more than six consecutive hours, she was eight years old. By the time she was nine, she was taking two different medications for sleep issues and we were still struggling.

If we could just leave Carly alone when she isn't sleeping, it would be one thing. But her sleeplessness also frequently involves pain or behaviors that are disruptive and destructive to her and to her environment. If we don't intervene and try to facilitate her relaxation, various complications arise which can include: bleeding feet and knees from the friction of hip rocking, severe muscle spasms and cramps, foot and ankle growth problems, spinal alignment issues, sore teeth and jaws from excessive grinding, torn pajamas, soaking wet clothing and bedding, various types of messes you'd rather not visualize or smell, broken furnishings, a hole in the sheet rock, and so on.

Left to her own devices, Carly can get stuck in behaviors that keep her awake for days at a time. The prolonged lack of sleep can then contribute to seizures for her as well. As a result, these situations demand much from us physically, mentally, and emotionally. Sometimes she requires physical restraint; other times we are problem solving which strategies are most likely to relieve her pain or calm her manic episodes of sensory-addictive behavior. Many of these times, we have been at our "wits' end" and raw with emotion.

One night when Carly was just starting to become mobile, we awoke to the extended sounds of something crashing. Upon entering her room, we found the little rascal standing at one of her windows holding onto the wooden blinds while pushing and pulling them back and forth wildly. Carly thought it was hilarious. Larry and I, not so much. That raw, middle-of-the-night emotion kicked in immediately. Problem solving mode was triggered promptly after that. Just imagine spouses debating their best strategic opinions when they are well rested, in a good mood, and facing a creative household redecorating project that will be exciting to see completed. Now imagine that same debate in the context of sleep deprivation, really irritated moods, and facing a project that is bound to end in something expensive, unattractive, and constantly reminding us of how much our life is not the way we hoped it would be.

In the middle of that night we were moving very heavy furniture and screaming at each other. The next day, a three-foot by four-foot sheet of plywood was nailed over one of the windows. That window remained boarded up and a tall dresser stood in front of the other window for a couple of years until a more significant construction project remodeled the entire room to address safety, noise, and sensory issues.

Larry and I have spent many nights tag-teaming our turns with her, each of us lasting only a couple of hours at a time before shaking with frustration. Each of us has spent long periods of time laying awake, often in tears, crying out in complete desperation and wondering why there seems to be no end to Carly's suffering and ours. No answers, no solutions to the problems, no relief for Carly's pain, no peace for her sensory cravings, no time to cuddle next to each other in our own bed, no freedom for us, no end in sight.

We asked every "Why?" question that could be asked. We agonized, "Why is this going on so long, Lord?" We would always circle back around to the same question wondering, "What are we missing, Lord?" Constantly I (Lisa) would suspect something must be lacking in me or us. If we had more faith, less sin, greater wisdom, or better ideas about how to help Carly then we thought things would change and improve. Many nights Larry would walk through the entire house covering our family with prayer before the bedtime routine would begin. Needless to say, we both wrestled mightily on every level. The father of lies could quickly get a foothold in our doubts and frustrations and resentment pulling us further and further from God and each other.

Another night was particularly memorable. Carly was about eight years old and I was begging God again to show me if there was some unconfessed sin in my life getting in the way of His help and our relief. I wondered if I lacked some special kind of faith. I asked God to make me more open to what nature of character building He must want to do in me. I begged God to fill me with more faith. I waged warfare against any spirits that were coming against the Lord's power to release healing and peace. Again and again I would ask the Lord to show me if this challenge was designed to help me grow. I suspected that I was being tested and that the Lord was teaching me patience and spiritual disciplines like prayer. So as Carly continued in her own restlessness and tears, I buried my face in her pillow and screamed.

The answer came to me at about 3:30 that morning. Out of the cacophony of thoughts and emotions whirling through my mind, one simple statement came to rest. It's not about you, Lisa. It's about Me. It wasn't really a voice, but it was unmistakably God. As I lay there, God started methodically walking me through some important truths. My thoughts were quickly sifted and sorted and brought into stilled focus.

Romans 8:1 says, *"There is no condemnation for those who live in Christ."* Satan is the accuser. Those shaming, accusatory tones I was hearing were not from the Lord.

Satan would tell us that we needed to own the problem—to take charge and fix it. God encourages us to utilize the resources he makes available but insists that we recognize His ultimate authority to handle the outcome. We had done everything within our power and control to help Carly. We had accessed every possible medical resource and genuinely pursued Biblical teachings about healing. God floated a timely verse across my mind:

> *"For my thoughts are not your thoughts, neither are your ways my ways," declares the Lord. "As the heavens are higher than the earth, so are my ways higher then your ways and my thoughts than your thoughts. As the rain and the snow*

come down from heaven, and do not return to it without watering the earth and making it bud and flourish, so that it yields seed for the sower and bread for the eater, so is my word that goes out from my mouth: It will not return to me empty, but will accomplish what I desire and achieve the purpose for which I sent it."
ISAIAH 55:8-11

There would be great significance to God's timing when He provided relief, or didn't. In terms of human logic, it didn't make sense that God would allow such stress and fatigue and pain to continue. With the big picture perspective that God has, I could be certain that it did make sense.

I also finally allowed myself to see that Jesus would want me to embrace the very next opportunity for a nap. If that was weakness, God would use it as an opportunity to show His own strength.

And here was the clincher God showed me: He is not as narrow-minded as I am. My concerns usually revolve around myself: Why am I uncomfortable? Why is God letting this happen to me? What should I be doing more of or differently? Wouldn't my life be so much easier and more available to do ministry if God would heal Carly of her sleep challenges?

I pondered all these rather narcissistic questions. And then God reminded me, "Something much **bigger than you** is going on here." Philippians 2:13 says, *"for it is God who works in you to will and to act according to his good purpose."* In other words, as long as I was trying to live my life yielded to Him, I could trust that what was going on had to do with things far beyond me. With that reminder I could acknowledge my own sin, my own need for character regeneration, my own cravings for rest and wholeness. I could see that God cares about all of those things. But I could also see that His perspective and purposes are much more complex than mine.

There is freedom and release in remembering that God is squeezing all kinds of great stuff out of all kinds of people through this situation. It involves a lot more than just what is going on inside of me. There is great relief and exciting hope in remembering that many lives are being impacted for the Kingdom as a result of this situation. Doctors, teachers, teenagers and adults who help us care for Carly, friends, family, and people we don't even know are aware of the struggle. Many of these people have experienced our weaknesses first hand, and those weaknesses are even more glaring after several days of stressful, sleepless nights. Fatigue has intensified our existing tendencies to run behind schedule, drive too fast, forget things, procrastinate things, talk too much, say the wrong thing, stir up a critical spirit, and want to control things—and we mean really want to control things! If nothing else, total exhaustion has forced us to depend less on ourselves and more on God.

So it is that when we are unable to keep up with our usual standards of function due to fatigue, God has shown up. Others may not be aware, but we certainly know in our own spirits when God has accomplished in us something we could not have accomplished within ourselves. It has been inspiring to us to share a sense of Paul's experience of praying about his own plaguing struggles. In the midst of Paul's insufficiencies, God was sufficient.

> *Three times I pleaded with the Lord to take (the thorn) away from me. But he said to me, "My grace is sufficient for you, for my power is made perfect in weakness." Therefore I will boast all the more gladly about my weaknesses, so that Christ's power may rest on me. That is why, for Christ's sake, I delight in weaknesses, in insults, in hardships, in persecutions, in difficulties. For when I am weak, then I am strong.*
> 2 CORINTHIANS 12:8-10

Even when God doesn't respond the way we hope, He is at work ensuring that good comes out of the situation. We may never witness the fruit of all the nighttime strife but we can trust that there will, in fact, be fruit. Somewhere in the midst of our struggle, God is working. In fact, like Bruce and Barb, we are coming to appreciate that often God is working **because** we are struggling.

When we are struggling with frustration and fatigue in our situation, we are learning to pray that God will give us His Kingdom perspective on things. We don't have to know the specifics of His plans. Our interpretation of the circumstances is based on so much less information than what God has. When we reconsider our situation in light of a Divine Plan, then the spirits of anger and hopelessness began to loose their grip.

When Jesus faced imminent persecution and death on the cross, he hinted about a kingdom perspective that would make sense of His suffering.

> *And he said to them, "I have eagerly desired to eat this Passover with you before I suffer. For I tell you, I will not eat of it again until it finds fulfillment in the kingdom of God."*
> LUKE 22:14

Hours later in the garden of Gethsemane, He ultimately surrendered his own hopes to God's will. This was not an easy process even for Jesus. He was so anxious that His sweat was like drops of blood falling to the ground (Luke 22:51). Nonetheless, Jesus knew God's plans to be completely trustworthy because Jesus knew His Father. He could endure every rip of his flesh, every horrific blow, every agonizing smash of the hammer because He allowed God's vision of the bigger picture to capture the focus of His heart. He allowed Himself —mind, body, heart, and will—to be conformed to that vision.

The ability to maintain a Kingdom perspective is developed in us by the Holy Spirit and also by our dwelling in the Word of God. We must get to know the character and habits of our Lord so that we have a model for our own responses and an intimate understanding of our Creator's heart. We have to make choices, moment by moment, about how we are going to think, what we are going to believe, and how we are going to respond. This is the hard work of a persevering Christ-follower, and it is an effort that bears exciting fruit within us and around us.

Set your minds on things above, not on earthly things.
COLOSSIANS 3:2

Seeking a Kingdom perspective is liberating! Pursuing an understanding of God's heart and mind for our struggles frees us from getting stuck looking inwardly. We are released to see that God's work, while intimately concerned with our best, also seeks what is best for the larger community of people He loves. As we recognize ourselves as part of the larger Body of Christ, we appreciate our significance with a whole new perspective. Instead of asking, "Why, God?" we find ourselves asking, "Why not?"

It Helps to Stop and Look at the Rocks

Most Saturday nights are a special "date night" for us. We go out to eat and sometimes do a little shopping, catch a movie, go for a walk around a lake, or play a game of cards at a coffee shop. But no matter who sees us or what effect it has on the temperature of our food, the pattern is always the same. Every time the meal is placed on the table in front of us, Larry reaches for my hand and we pray. On many occasions our waiter has returned to check our satisfaction with the meal and we haven't even tasted it yet!

You see, we don't come into that moment lightly. It's not a traditional blessing over the meal. This is a moment when we feel interconnected by a very complicated life within the arms of our loving God. In that moment when we look into each other's eyes right before we bow our heads, there is an understanding. We share a common hope that in this moment God will breathe some fresh air into us individually and as a couple. And when we reopen our eyes, each of us sees something reassuring in the other as if looking into the eyes of Jesus Himself. We have a sense that even when we walk back in that door at home and everything is the same as when we left, life is good because we aren't alone. God is with us and He's given us each other.

It hasn't always been this way for us. We've experienced some painful times of separation in our relationship. There were some years when the walls were invisible but thick. There had been one particular season when we were hanging on bare threads of hope that there would ever be a tender intimacy and romance between us again.

On the other side of those early days in our marriage, we can rejoice in knowing that hope in Christ never disappointed us. God had proven time and again His ability to "*do more than all we ask or imagine, according to his power that is at work within us*" (Ephesians 3:20). We can look back on our relationship and be amazed, even excited, to see what unexpected depths of love God has brought us into. Remembering how God has brought strength to our marriage and how He has been present in the many layers of Carly's situation renews our hope that He will come through for us again in the future.

It is helpful, even necessary, to remember how God has proven Himself faithful in the past. As God keeps adding to our experiences of His faithfulness, our confidence grows. We are reassured of the truth that there is hope in the journey.

When the nation of Israel had finished crossing the Jordan River, the Lord told Joshua to construct a memorial.

> "*Choose twelve men from among the people, one from each tribe, and tell them to take up twelve stones from the middle of the Jordan from right where the priests stood and to carry them over with you and put them down at the place where you stay tonight.*"
> JOSHUA 4:2-3

Why did God insist on this? The Israelites wondered the same thing so Joshua explained.

> *He said to the Israelites, "In the future when your descendants ask their fathers, 'What do these stones mean?' tell them, 'Israel crossed the Jordan on dry ground.' For the Lord your God dried up the Jordan before you until you had crossed over. The Lord your God did to the Jordan just what he had done to the Red Sea when he dried it up before us until we*

*had crossed over. He did this so that all the peoples of the
earth might know that the hand of the Lord is powerful
and so that you might always fear the Lord your God."*
JOSHUA 4:21-24

God knows our nature to need reminders of His faithfulness.
Throughout history God's people have celebrated His presence
and care for them at significant times. The Old Testament
feasts celebrated God at work. Ultimately, the Last Supper
commemorates the new covenant we have with God through
Jesus' suffering, death, and resurrection. Our celebration of
communion is the obedient response to a knowing God who
insisted in Luke 22:19, *"Do this in remembrance of me."*

Today, our family has several thick three-ring binders overflowing
with years' worth of "Carly Updates." Those email updates were
sent to family and friends who prayed with diligence and hope for
Carly. They are our historical record of God's faithfulness to us.
We see that stack of binders as our pile of rocks stacked up on the
Promised Land side of many steps we have taken through a faith-
dependent journey. Each "Carly Update" stands as one of many
stones in our memorial. It will tell generations to come about
God's awesome work sustaining our family through seemingly
impossible times and His power in releasing developmental
progress in Carly that few expected in her lifetime. We can stop
and look at our memories as often as necessary when we need
reassurance that God is worthy of our hope. Over and over again
God has done amazing and unexpected things.

How exciting to know we can experience our own Jordan
crossings and have opportunities to build living memorials to
celebrate God's goodness to us. We love to stop often and look
at those rocks!

We Can Expect the Unexpected

We need only look to Jesus to realize that God is in the business
of doing unexpected things.

- God promised a Messiah. Nobody expected a baby, and certainly not Emmanuel lying in a manger! He was rejected, ignored, threatened, and scorned yet He embodied the Way, the Truth, and the Life.
- Jesus lived the humble life of a carpenter, hung out with ordinary people, and taught God's Law with profound accuracy, creativity, and influence. Nobody expected that kind of person to perform countless miracles, befriend sinners and heal them, then even to forgive sins. Not only did he demonstrate pure godliness, he demanded that people be willing to give up everything they loved to follow him.
- Jesus was beaten beyond recognition and near death. Nobody expected God's chosen people to treat God that way. No one expected Him to survive the torture. No one expected him to endure further suffering nailed to a cross.
- Jesus died. Nobody expected the Messiah to die. They expected the Messiah to be a different kind of king. No one expected that a mere man could become the scapegoat for the sins of all humanity.
- After Jesus died, He came back to those who loved Him. Nobody expected He would return, then ascend to heaven, and leave the Holy Spirit as His eternal comforting and guiding presence. His painful death and subsequent resurrection, together, assured that Christ could dwell within those who believed. By their faith, believers received the gift of eternal salvation.

None of it looked like a good thing at first. God did things through Jesus that defied all expectations. But when the Kingdom perspective was revealed, it was all Good News!

The Apostle Paul was on an influential mission to tell the world about that Good News but he was thrown in prison. No one expected that to be a good thing either.

Not once. Not twice. But many times and for many years, things didn't look good for Paul or for the spreading of the Gospel. His friends vigilantly prayed asking God to restore Paul's freedom. Though Paul was repeatedly returned to prison, He wrote letters thanking believers for their faith, for hoping with Him that God's plans would be fulfilled despite what seemed like endless obstacles. Those letters became an important part of the inspired Word of God available to millions of people for future generations. Like memorial stones.

Did Paul ever expect that such significant fruit would come from the ministry of his letters? Paul did expect his ministry to take him places across land and sea. Paul never reached many of those places but his words still do today on the pages of Scripture because they were words breathed by God Himself through Paul's serving hand. What an unexpected way for us to receive the Good News!

Paul did know God's loving power to do immeasurably more than we ask or imagine. That is why he was constantly encouraging his fellow believers. He regularly saw reasons to remain hopeful despite persecution, imprisonment, and near constant suffering. Rather than allowing his circumstances to discourage him or those praying for him, he prayed for maturing faith and embraced memories of God's faithfulness in the past. Consider the encouragement of Paul's kingdom perspective:

> *I consider that our present sufferings are not worth comparing with the glory that will be revealed in us.*
> ROMANS 8:18

Paul includes this in the midst of an encouraging discussion about the power of the Spirit within us.

> *The Spirit himself testifies with our spirit that we are God's children. Now if we are children, then we are heirs—heirs of God and co-heirs with Christ, if indeed we share in his sufferings in order that we may also share in his glory. I consider that our present sufferings are not worth comparing with the glory that will be revealed in us.*
> *In the same way, the Spirit helps us in our weakness. We do not know what we ought to pray, but the Spirit himself intercedes*

for us with groans that words cannot express. And he who searches our hearts knows the mind of the Spirit, because the Spirit intercedes for the saints in accordance with God's will. And we know that in all things God works for the good of those who love him, who have been called according to his purpose.
ROMANS 8:16-17 AND 26-28

Paul recognized that there was nothing more important than remaining eternally in God's presence. No amount of hardship, vulnerability, or danger can separate us from it. He also pointed to Jesus' interceding spirit who perfectly knows the will of God and what we should pray for. When our affections are focused on Almighty God, our hearts conform to His will and victory over all our suffering ultimately ends in glory to God.

No, in all these things we are more than conquerors through him who loved us. For I am convinced that neither death nor life, neither angels nor demons, neither the present nor the future, nor any powers, neither height nor depth, nor anything else in all creation, will be able to separate us from the love of God that is in Christ Jesus our Lord.
ROMANS 8:37-39

Is that the loving God you know?

Is Your God Big Enough?

There is great temptation to give up hoping for miracles. It often seems easier, or at least less emotionally risky, to give up hoping that our situation will ever change. After all, why leave ourselves vulnerable to disappointment by hoping God will do something earth-shaking? But what if anticipating the remarkable, exciting, surprising, and life-lifting things God has planned is exactly what He expects us to do? What if God wants us to hold on to a dramatically magnified understanding of His love for us and His power to do something marvelous, even unexpected, with our circumstances?

During our most hopeless moments and seasons, it has been critical for us to refocus our attention on who God is. Recognizing God's power, perfection, and all-consuming love reassures us that He has the authority and compassion to handle everything about our situation. God's desire is for things to turn out well.

Come with us into history to rediscover God's holiness. Bring with you your longings for hope, your numb emotions, your confusion about your life situation, your loneliness, your fatigue, your feelings of being overwhelmed, your aching heart. Bring your concerns about whether things will ever change— whether they will ever get better, easier, happier, less intense, exciting, or comfortable again.

Thousands of years ago, the prophet Isaiah was given a vision of God Almighty. Read it slowly, even a couple of times, and imagine the scene:

> *In the year King Uzziah died, I saw the Lord. He was sitting on a lofty throne, and the train of His robe filled the Temple. Hovering around Him were mighty seraphim, each with six wings. With two wings they covered their faces, with two they covered their feet, and with the remaining two they flew. In a great chorus they sang, "Holy, holy, holy is the Lord Almighty! The whole earth is filled with His glory!" The glorious singing shook the Temple to its foundations, and the entire sanctuary was filled with smoke.*
> ISAIAH 6:1-4

Now go back and read it once more. This time, focus especially on those things that demonstrate God's power, magnificence, and transcendence. He sat on a throne that was lofty. What does that look like? The train of his robe quite literally filled the Temple. Suspended in the air all round His being were winged spiritual beings. Does the significance of their covering themselves have anything to do with their need to cover unworthiness, their sense of awe in being in God's presence? The enormous choir sang in deeply affectionate worship. The thing that struck them most about the Lord was His holiness. They were so consumed by God's greatness that they sang about it over and over again. Their singing was so intense that the very foundations of the Temple were significantly agitated. The smoke that penetrated the sanctuary may have been dust, maybe even smoke from the fires of friction and heat created by all that shaking going on!

Go ahead. Re-read it and consider that this God Isaiah was seeing is your God too. Does the mental image you have of God today come anything close to this? Have you taken time lately to consider the true greatness of your God's power and strength? His purity and perfection? His everlasting and passionate love for you? Have you pondered His ability and willingness to transcend all of creation to dwell in YOUR midst?

We worship the one true God who is all-powerful, all-knowing, always loving, and only capable of good things. Do you really believe that? Is your understanding and appreciation of God big enough? It's one thing to believe there is a God. It's another thing to have an appropriate perspective about that God's sovereignty and perfectly loving nature.

Perhaps you've had experiences like us that have shaken your appreciation for who God really is. At times, the passion of our devotion to God has cooled. Or we have become so comfortable in our relationship with Jesus that we have neglected to appreciate Him with the awe and reverence that God deserves. We sometimes develop and dwell in some fairly negative attitudes towards God: resentment, impatience, and even indifference.

Despite our heart's tendency to shift like the sands, and regardless of the evolution of our problems, God is always the same. His holiness never changes, never diminishes, never fails. It is entirely and everlastingly dependable. God's character is constant no matter what chaos our life is in.

So if you find yourself in a place like that, where your hope is dim, consider the possibility that you are having a crisis of understanding the full nature of who God is. This may be a good season for you to spend time meditating on the character of God.

It may also be helpful to explore the Scriptures, searching for ways God has revealed Himself to His people throughout history:

He was present in the Garden of Eden (Genesis 3:8),

He showed Himself to Moses in the burning bush (Exodus 3:4) and passing by the cleft in the rock (Exodus 33:22-23),

He led the Egyptians with pillars of fire and cloud (Exodus 13:21-22),

He filled and surrounded the Tabernacle (Exodus 40:34-38),

He gave visions to the prophets (Isaiah 9:6-7,),

He sent Jesus (Luke 1:31-33)!

He gave visions to the disciples (Acts 9:1-19, Revelation 4).

No doubt you have experiences of God's presence too. But have you noticed them? Do you see your story as a continuation of a Divine history unfolding? You can and you should! God's desire to be present in our midst has not changed.

If your hopefulness about your circumstances is shaky, even if you are completely depressed and have lost hope altogether, God has enough grace for that. Psalm 139:6 says that God knows us so intimately that our minds cannot grasp it. Nothing is hidden from Him about your situation, not even our thoughts and feelings. He is thinking about us constantly, even when we are not thinking about Him.

Perhaps you can relate to our experience of frustration during sleepless nights. Those have been tedious and overwhelming times of trying to understand God's plans and purposes. We tend to feel hopeless when we can't rationalize a situation and make meaning out of it. That, by the way, is how surrender enters the picture. It is not necessary that we understand our situation. It is only necessary that God understands it.

Ask God to magnify your understanding of His greatness. Fifteen minutes of prayerful meditation on what the Bible says about God is a good way to let Him begin stirring up your perspectives. It may take several days or weeks. But it is so worth taking the time! Give God the opportunity to expand your appreciation of who He is and He will be faithful to you.

It is one of His many and good gifts. God is not an image you conjure up on your own. God is not something you can begin to understand through your own willpower. The kind of insight you need is available only by God's divine revelation. Ask Him to open your eyes to see Him anew.

Because of the nature of who God is, we can put our hopes and dreams in His care. He is able and willing to respond in some way to your situation. He has enough power, enough wisdom, enough love to handle it. No situation is too complicated, too challenging, or too insignificant for His perfect intervention. He may not handle it the way you want or expect Him to. But His response will be the perfect one because He perfectly understands the past, present, and future of your situation—because **He is God**. He will take care of it in the most perfect way for the benefit of His glory and with a love for you that is wider, longer, and deeper than what you can comprehend.

Are you ready for that? Because your God really is big enough if you are willing to surrender your impossibilities to His God-sized possibilities. Let your hopeless moments get caught up in the anticipation of what your compassionate, creative, and powerful God will do. Be willing to submit your own expectations to the authority of the Almighty. Cling to hope with all your might, keep your eyes wide open to see Him at work in unexpected ways in your midst. Let Him surprise your socks off!

TO EXPERIENCE HOPE...

ANTICIPATE THE SURPRISES OF GOD'S LOVE

Now to him who is able to do immeasurably more than all we ask or imagine, according to his power that is at work within us, to him be the glory in the church and in Christ Jesus throughout all generations, for ever and ever! Amen.
EPHESIANS 3:20-21

Practice these things while praying for God to fill you with Hope:
• Consider: What might God's kingdom perspective look like in your present circumstances?
• Think of a time when things you were worried or anxious about turned out better than you expected. In what specific ways was the result different than you anticipated it would be?
• Start making a list of specific ways God has shown Himself faithful to you over the years. Add to it every time another event worth celebrating comes to mind. Eased burdens and reconciled relationship should go on your list too.

Lord, I am so grateful for the reminder that you are always sovereign, sufficient, and compassionate. You care about my suffering. Every detail of my situation matters to you. Nothing is too complicated, too challenging, or too insignificant for your perfect intervention. Help me to trust in your higher understanding and ways. Help me to see that within the great depths of your love for me, there are wonderful surprises in store because you can do immeasurably more than all I could ever ask or imagine. Keep me coming back to your Word, Lord, because that is where you will teach me about your promises and about what your Kingdom perspective looks like. Help me to keep my affections and hopes focused on you so that everything going on in my life can be worked for good in your Kingdom. AMEN

Chapter 11:
JOY — *How do I experience it?*

A couple of years ago, a close friend of ours came to life with ALS (a devastating, life-taking illness also known as Lou Gehrig's disease). Yes, you read that correctly — came to life. As we watched Chuck's physical body deteriorating, we saw Chuck and his family coming to life with a level of fullness that few people ever achieve. How did they do it? That's a question worth pondering because, if you had seen them as we did, you would have wanted what they had.

This was a family that, admittedly, had a lot of baggage. Anyone with a similar history may have become bitter that God would take this young man of fifty-nine from a wife, three children with loving spouses, and seven grandchildren who absolutely adored him at the very time when life was coming together for them in exciting ways. During the years when his children were growing up, Chuck was an alcoholic. Thankfully, Chuck knew the Lord for twenty years. He was living a road of recovery that was thrilling to him and those who knew him. Yet now, when Chuck was finally enjoying a growing intimacy with his Savior and the relationships in his life were thriving and strong, his body was growing weaker and weaker by the day.

Rather than lingering in disappointment, Chuck chose to live his last days in the joy of the Lord. And his joyfulness was a contagious thing. Friends would gather one evening every week to pray with Chuck and his wife, Maryann. And each week, people would marvel at their authenticity. They were very candid about ways in which they were struggling. They didn't hide the anguish of their hearts. Whether there were tough decisions to make about moving out of the home where they raised their children or guilty feelings about needing some privacy, they were willing to lay out their vulnerabilities before God and their friends. And all the while, people wanted to be around this couple. Despite Chuck's rapidly deteriorating health, the fragrance of the joy of Christ was in that place and people were drawn to it. We were excited when our schedule would allow us to join the prayer group and disappointed when it didn't.

You see, Chuck's family didn't wallow in their suffering. There were often tears and intense emotion but they didn't linger there. Woven through every conversation was a spirit of authentic thankfulness. This was a family who took nothing for granted. They savored good memories and reflected often on the amazing redemption and restoration they had been given by God. On several occasions, we heard Maryann proclaim her deep gratitude to God for restoring *"the years the locusts (had) eaten."* Joel 2:25

Chuck's family also found a lot to laugh about. They understood what Scripture says about laughter. *"A cheerful heart is good medicine,"* says Proverbs 17:22 *"but a crushed spirit dries up the bones."*

Chuck embraced his opportunity to live the Apostle Paul's secret.

> *"I know what it is to be in need, and I know what it is to have plenty. I have learned the secret of being content in any and every situation...I can do everything through him who gives me strength."*
> PHILIPPIANS 4:12-13

When his body and voice denied him the ability to contribute in any other way, Chuck would enthusiastically remind the rest of us discouraged onlookers "I can still read the Word, and I can always be praying." For Larry and I, that was humbling and reassuring and incredibly exciting. To know that Chuck was one of a few people who quite literally talked with Jesus **every day** for Carly was a gift that showed fruit in her sleep and development as well as our courage. Chuck's disability contributed to Carly's ability.

Chuck recognized our mutual and utter dependence on God and an overwhelming sense of gratitude poured out of him. And do you know what it looked like to the rest of us? Joy. In fact, the picture of joy that Chuck and his family gave people for two years is a gift we will all benefit from for the rest of our lives. In addition to the powerful testimony this man had about how God had snatched him from a pit of alcoholism, his legacy was the joy and encouragement of Christ that poured out of him onto every life he touched.

Did you catch that? Chuck's legacy wasn't what a great man Chuck was. Chuck's legacy was his joy in what a great God, God is!

Thankfulness Makes Room for Joy

There is an undeniable interconnection between joy and thankfulness because that's the way God designed it to be. And He makes no exception for times of difficulty. God insists that we deliberately choose where we will put the focus of our attention regardless of our circumstances.

Paul articulated God's design in these ways in his letters to the early Christ followers:

> *Be joyful **always**; pray continually; give thanks **in all circumstances**, for **this is God's will for you** in Christ Jesus.*
> 1 THESSALONIANS 5:28

> *Let the peace of Christ rule in your hearts, since as members of one body you were called to peace. And **be thankful**! Let the word of Christ dwell in you richly as you teach and admonish one another with all wisdom, and as you sing psalms, hymns, and spiritual songs **with gratitude in your hearts to God**. And whatever you do, whether in word or deed, do it all in the name of the Lord Jesus, **giving thanks** to God the Father through Him.*
> COLOSSIANS 3:15-17

> *"Rejoice in the Lord always. I will say it again: Rejoice! Let your gentleness be evident to all. The Lord is near.*

*Do not be anxious about anything, but **in everything,** by prayer and petition, **with thanksgiving,** present your requests to God. And the peace of God, which transcends all understanding, will guard your hearts and your minds in Christ Jesus. Finally brothers, whatever is true, whatever is noble, whatever is right, whatever is pure, whatever is lovely, whatever is admirable —if anything is excellent or praiseworthy—think about such things.*
Philippians 4:4-7 (Emphasis ours)

God never made thankfulness optional and His principles remain true for us today. What is to be the focus of our joy? The Lord. In what spirit are we exhorted to come before God? A spirit of thanksgiving. What parts of all the many things going on in our lives are we supposed to dwell on and meditate? The true, noble, right, pure, lovely, admirable, excellent, and praiseworthy stuff!

Does that mean we can't acknowledge the things that make us sad, angry, disappointed, worried, hurt, or doubtful? No. The Bible is full of people recounting their pain and suffering before God. The Psalms, Lamentations, and Paul's letters are some of the places we can go to find resonance with other godly but struggling people and appreciate how they got through it all by the love and grace of God. We are simply not to dwell there. We are not to fixate on those things that rob of us of our joy. We are to keep turning away from the darkness and deliberately choosing to walk boldly on the path that takes us into the Light!

Do you find yourself arguing that sometimes it's just not possible to be thankful in every single circumstance? When there have seemed to be no ways or reasons to stay thankful, we have found ourselves thinking things like "well, at least we don't have it as bad as that other person or that other family." It can help to escape into someone else's harsh reality. It allows us, if even for a little while, to forget about our own. It was God's Divine timing for me that I was trying to hide from my own life's overwhelming realities when I read Corrie ten Boom's book, *The Hiding Place.* I read parts of it to Larry too. Corrie gave us a renewed appreciation for the unconscionable suffering people endured during the Holocaust. Our hearts ached anew for people who are persecuted but our convictions about the need for a thankful heart was also reaffirmed. Corrie and her sister, Betsie, endured the unthinkable and remained thankful.

There are times, however, when the last thing we want is to think about how much worse somebody else has it. We want someone or something to acknowledge, even validate, the great difficulty we are in. We really don't want to hear that someone else is worse off.

Larry and I find it difficult to admit how often we have felt sorry for ourselves since Carly was born. Sleep deprivation is a partial explanation for magnified existing tendencies towards self-centeredness but it is no excuse for a prolonged "woe is me" attitude. Even Alex and Erin have been overcome with frustration a time or two. One night, Alex tearfully admitted how she resented that "some people's lives just seem so much more low maintenance compared to us." During that conversation, we all expressed frustration with how many of our family plans have to revolve around Carly. Each of us admitted to being angry whenever returning home after being away. Whether the girls had a play date with a friend or we were coming back from a vacation, we had all experienced intensely deflating feelings of being thrust back into an undesirable reality. We find ourselves coveting what others have or resenting what we don't have. Jealousy steals joy.

We also tend to fester about our financial situation. We live with regrets about having left ourselves without a safety cushion and feel resentment over the loss of our retirement to all of the unexpected expenses. There are plenty of reasons and opportunities for us to complain, criticize, and feel guilty. All of this lack of thankfulness is a cancer to joy-filled living.

We are thankful to have had the Lord sear a mind set of thankfulness on our hearts even before Carly was born. (It is no coincidence that God does some preparation with us ahead of time for the different seasons we will pass through.) Because we had already been learning certain lessons about thankfulness, we started life with Carly already on the lookout for God's fingerprints on her life. We were better prepared to look back and forward with appreciation of His constant presence.

Two particularly defining moments that helped move us in the direction of joyful living are worth mentioning here.

The first came at a time of crisis early in our marriage. Both of us were brewing in resentment and grief. Each of us felt guilty for our own roles in a problem we were having but I (Lisa) had a particular tendency to cling to my anger and dwell in all the reasons why it was justified. With each day that passed the distance between us grew and my mind was consumed with negative emotion. The weight of the issues felt unbearable.

Then one day God used a song on the radio to take me to that portion of Philippians 4:8 that instructs us to think about the true, noble, pure, lovely, admirable, excellent, and praiseworthy things. Never before had the message of God's Word pierced into my heart and mind the way it did that day. I didn't come willingly to that challenge but God softened my heart to recognize its value and my need to be obedient.

I began memorizing Philippians 4:8 and singing the once very popular song based on that verse. I sang it a hundred times a day if I sang it once. I sang it every time I felt my mind spiraling out of control, wrapping itself around all the unanswered questions, fears, and bitterness. I have tears in my eyes even now remembering what a sorrowful time that was in my life but it was my first significant opportunity to begin learning how to turn away from the darkness and stay pointed in the direction of Joy.

The second defining moment involved a friend and what started out as a mysterious lunch date. She invited me to lunch hinting she had something important to talk with me about. As it turns out, that lunch emerges on my "Top 10 Most Painful Conversations" list.

In the middle of a restaurant, I dried the tears streaming down my cheeks as I listened. My friend carefully began describing examples she'd witnessed of my critical spirit and my perpetual need to evaluate things and point out how things could be better. I would even make sarcastic jokes about how something or somebody had fallen short. She suggested that my high expectations, while well intentioned, could be intimidating or leave people feeling disrespected or even offended. She challenged me to consider that I was chipping away at my husband's sense of confidence and self-respect while alienating us from each other. She urged me to set down criticism and pick up gratitude. "Thankfulness is the opposite of criticism, you know," she added. "The more time you spend looking for things you can genuinely be thankful about, the less time you'll have for judging them."

Initially, my defenses kicked in and I felt misunderstood. I was angry with her for judging and misunderstanding me. After all, didn't my tendency to be crabby have something to do with sleep deprivation? And wasn't my passion for excellence part of what made me successful in my career? After all, our business had literally won awards with clients because of our diligence for quality service. I considered it a bit of a gift that I could see opportunities to improve things in almost every area of life. Things could always be made even better than they were. But in the pain of what she said, my heart knew there was truth.

When I cooled off, I recognized that I probably needed someone willing to be bold with me. I admitted to God that I couldn't do it without His help and asked Him to start changing me right away. I prefer not to admit it's been over ten years since that memorable lunch because I'm often doubtful that the progress I've made towards Christ-likeness in that area is sufficient. But our marriage experienced powerful changes in a more positive direction as a result. In fact, Larry and I have never been quite the same since. And thankfully so, because the strongest of all possible marriages was precisely what we needed when Carly was born. Thanks be to God for seeing the big picture and helping us get ready to be a team on a whole new level!

Larry and I have been re-inspired by memories like these over the years and, consequently, continue developing a lifestyle of thankfulness. Regularly journaling in the "Carly Updates" about both the blessings and prayer needs we have helps us to keep things in perspective. Intentionally acknowledging God's blessings heightens our awareness of the encouraging things that are happening. Noting prayer needs keeps us humble before our friends and family while also keeping us surrendered at Jesus' feet. If there is any temptation to take credit for progress or wallow in our suffering, taking frequent account of God's goodness and our great dependency on Him helps us maintain integrity and humility.

We don't write "Carly Updates" nearly as often anymore as we did in the early days of Carly's diagnosis and therapies. Nowadays, discouragement, dissatisfaction, and discontentment are common triggers for the distribution of an update because writing an update holds us accountable to reflecting on our life situation with a perspective of gratitude. In the process of sitting down and writing out the things going on that are worth celebrating, we are given opportunity to dwell on the true, noble, pure, lovely, admirable, excellent, and praiseworthy things. In that process, God encourages us and shifts our attitudes.

Following a similar structure during times of prayer with our small groups has proven equally fruitful. At times, our small group bible study discussions could either get stuck in praying about crises or people tended to share only the most surface-level issues going on in their families. People might even be hesitant to tell about the good things going on for fear of sounding prideful. But, when people are courageous enough to share their very real struggles while also being challenged to acknowledge how God is releasing blessing in their family during any given week, many amazing things happen. Relational bonds grow deep. Forgiveness is released when sin is publicly confessed. God's goodness is more evident on our radar when we are on the lookout for positive things to be sharing with our small group. Joy is magnified when God's activity in our lives, both praiseworthy and challenging, is shared.

It is actually refreshing to know that we can follow God's design and He will do the work of molding us. When we choose to be thankful in obedience to Him, God increases our joy!

The Word of God Revives the Soul

God's Word supplies joy.

> *"The law of the Lord is perfect, reviving the soul... The precepts of the Lord are right, giving joy to the heart."*
> PSALM 19:7, 9

There it is. Another synergistic connection in Scripture.

In his final days, Chuck and his family literally saturated themselves in God's Word. During every prayer gathering, the group spent considerable time sharing about how the Scriptures were speaking into their circumstances. Our delight was in discovering what the Lord had to say and realizing how active and specific His precepts are in our lives! There is great power in the fellowship of Christ-centered believers who gather together to find delight in the Word of the Lord.

Finding private times for solitude with Jesus and our Bibles had become increasingly challenging. Although it should have been as simple as going to sit down in a chair for a few minutes, even that was difficult in our home. Every place with a chair was surrounded by activity and distraction. In addition, Lisa's list of things to do around our house had such a grip on her life that she rarely sat down except to drive the van or eat dinner. Getting up early was impossible when we were constantly up and down for most of the night!

It was some dear women in Lisa's Bible Study who helped me encourage her to follow her longings for a cozy chair and the sanctuary it embodied for her. So with my Christmas bonus we went shopping and started creating an out-of-the-way corner in our "piano room" for her to escape with Jesus.

The girls were of an age when getting them to practice piano was next to impossible unless a parent was sitting at attention and offering frequent encouragement, but our task lists were always beckoning. So when "I know I'm not right in the room honey, but I really am listening" wasn't good enough and since God was calling us to be still with Him, it seemed like an appropriate opportunity to multi-task!

The financial commitment we put into that chair, the desire to encourage our children in developing their musical gifts, and prompting from friends held me (Lisa) accountable to getting into a better posture with our kids and the Lord several times a week. Even as I was providing support and modeling worship for my kids, that chair became my sanctuary. As I sat reading my Bible, listening to their music, and prayerfully waiting for the promptings of the Holy Spirit, I felt fresh air blowing new wind into my sails.

It really wasn't "my" chair though. Larry was bringing his work on worship videos piano-side as well. Each of us has written some of this book while sitting in that chair.

Carly praises Jesus there now too. She bounces to the tunes while I play her a little worship set on the piano and many times she even sings. "Carly **sings**?" you ask with curiosity and even a little astonishment. Yes, Carly loves to sing. Only Jesus knows yet what her heart articulates to Him. But her participation with vocalizations, smiles, and hand-clapping cause joyous worship in our home where one day not so long ago there were mostly tears.

But, of course, it is not really about the chair. It's about the lifestyle we are developing that makes room for our relationship with the Lord to grow through worship, prayer, and Bible reading. A friend has reminded us, "it's not enough to just wave in the Lord's direction" in the scurry of life. God is not interested in religious habits. He wants a relationship. He wants our undivided attention and affection. That is worship — our part in the expression of love in that relationship.

The practice of worship and saturating ourselves in Scripture is entirely portable. Having "the chair" helped develop a routine for regular, intentional, focused time with Jesus. It didn't take long, however, before I could be sitting in the driver's seat waiting to pick up children or in a doctor's office waiting for an appointment and spend time in worship. Now all it takes is a Bible in my purse and a spirit attentive to God who is always available even when I am not. Larry goes almost nowhere without a Bible and his laptop. He may create more worship videos while waiting in his car to pick up kids from church activities than in any other place. Those waiting times of life are Divine opportunities for worship!

Every time and any place where we are directing a spirit of gratitude to God for who He is and what He is doing in our lives, we love Him. Every time and any place where we focus our passions and talents on the Creator who put them in us, we show our affection for Him. Every time and any place where we acknowledge God, we show respect for Him. Every time we open our Bible and really **listen** for Jesus' comfort, encouragement, guidance, and affection towards us, we honor and bless Him. And that brings Joy.

"Your words were found and I ate them, and your words became for me a joy and the delight of my heart."
JEREMIAH 15:16

In Old Testament times, God's presence could only be experienced by the chief priest from deep within the temple. His presence existed over the Arc of the Covenant under the arching wings of the cherubim. How thankful we are today that, because of Jesus' resurrection, each one of us can rest in the shelter of God's presence no matter who we are or where we are. Because of Christ's suffering and subsequent victory over death, we have the gift of the Holy Spirit. God is near, not far away. Because of our suffering on this journey with Carly, we are learning to receive and live within that nearness. And we will never be the same again.

Thank you, Jesus!

Loving Relationships are the Sweetest Joy
Few people can really appreciate what life is like for those of us facing health issues that have profoundly and forever revised the course of our lifestyle and lives. What a lonely thought! But the sad truth is that we are often very alone in the tedious daily grind

of caring for a loved one. Most other people cannot possibly understand what you have to deal with day in and day out.

Having experienced that sense of isolation and knowing that it can be difficult for others to relate to us, we have come to treasure even more our relationships with family and friends who try. Those people who continue to stand by us and love us, who have grace for us, are among God's most precious gifts. And they do bring joy indeed!

During the summer of 2000, I (Lisa) spent three days in northern Minnesota on a quiet retreat by myself. Upon returning home, I shared this journal entry with Larry to encourage him. I wanted Him to know that after two years of agonizing struggle with Carly, God was restoring my joy. I hoped that as I read, his joy would also be fanned into flame just being reminded of his preciousness to me.

> I have just been spending time on the end of the dock looking out over the rough water and listening to the wind. It is a hot day, the wind only slightly removing the weight of the heat from my skin. As I sat there in thankfulness for the moment, I imagined the voices of Alex and Erin breaking into the wind as they played in the waves. I thought about how different the moment would be with them in it—how lovingly I would look on them and how warmed I would be by their laughter while some part of me was still yearning for rest and solitude. It was at that moment I realized that the true sweetness of this solitude is in knowing that it is chosen not imposed. The very sweetest thing about sitting there is in recalling the list of memories God has given me of precious experiences and relationships in my life.
>
> I hear the sound of the Jet Ski and recall the many people we have shared fun weekends with here. I look over to the boat and am overcome by the countless days I have spent fishing with my sister and my parents—times that have shaped the "culture" of my family. I remember the touch from heaven I felt a few years ago while relaxing in a chaise on the beach while watching Alex and Erin dig in the sand. I

see Carly trying to crawl off of the blanket towards the sand only to fill her mouth with the texture of it. My mind stops abruptly in the Apostle Islands where I rest in Larry's arms in the moonlight. In a few minutes, I'm sitting on the bow of Second Gift feeling the wind in my face and the same sting of heat on my skin. I see God all over the place!

Dear God! Could it be that in this solitude, you are going to fill me with the tenderest of memories and show me that life is the journey from joy to joy with pauses for sorrow only to heighten the appeal of the next joy?

The sweetness of this moment is in knowing I love and am loved.

Relationships, first with Christ and then with others, are top priority with God. That doesn't mean He doesn't care about the details and logistics of our situation. But it does mean that He filters everything He does in caring for us through the lens of our relationships — our relationships with the people around us and our relationship with Him.

> *But may all who search for you be filled with joy and gladness.*
> *May those who love your salvation repeatedly shout, "God is great!"*
> PSALM 70:4

God understands when everything in your world has been turned upside down. He knows about the weight of all the added burdens you are bearing. He also understands that the stresses of coping with the thorny parts of life take a great toll on your relationships.

Are you holding a grudge because you and somebody else in your situation aren't on the same page about what's going on in your life crisis? Are you harboring some resentment about finances? Are you bitter about something that happened years ago that now feels integrally part of what's going on with the health or development of your loved one?

Jesus compares anger with a loved one to murder and says, *"anyone who is angry with his brother will be subject to judgment"*

(Matthew 5:22). He challenges those who love God to resolve everything between them before making any offering to God. Lacking respect and compassion for someone else's grieving process is a dangerous business. No difference of opinion about which medical treatment or therapeutic strategy to pursue is worth separation from God. Jesus insists we make it a top priority to restore broken relationships, which is consistent with His design that we love our neighbors like we love ourselves.

> *Therefore, if you are offering your gift at the altar and there remember that your brother has something against you, leave your gift there in front of the altar. First go and be reconciled to your brother; then come and offer your gift.*
> MATTHEW 5:23-24

Jesus urges *"settle matters quickly with your adversary"* (Matthew 5:25). Is there bitterness, misunderstanding, sin, lack of forgiveness, or hurt feelings going on in any of your relationships?

Get rid of it! Don't wait another minute. It's not worth it! Fall on your knees right now and beg God for His mercy over you and those others in your life who really matter. Then go. Go and make things right between you and your loved one. You are on the same team! Don't believe the lie that says, "this is as good as it gets."

Remember, God's desire is that you live in joy!

CULTIVATE A GRATEFUL HEART BEFORE GOD.

And whatever you do, whether in word or deed, do it all in the name of the Lord Jesus, giving thanks to God the Father through him.
COLOSSIANS 3:17

Practice these things while praying for God to increase your Joy:

- Consider the many opportunities you have throughout every day to pause and think about your parents, spouse, children, siblings, and friends — while driving in the car, showering, folding a loved one's laundry, washing dishes, laying awake in bed, making a meal, shaving, walking, TV commercial, working out, and so on.

- Consider how you can apply the precept of Philippians 4:8 to triggering moments. (This is not a time to ask God to change somebody or even help them. Certainly God wants us to come freely to him with those people's needs. But this time is simply and powerfully a time for gratitude.)

- Begin using more of these times to pray gratitude prayers over the people in your life. Commit to developing a habit of praying over each person in your family whenever something triggers a thought about them! For example, I pray for Carly as I walk back to the house after she leaves on the school bus. I may thank God for her teachers or for how independent she is becoming with her steps or that she waved good-bye to me.

When I help her with stretching exercises, I thank God for progress in the healing of her bones and for giving me time to spend helping with her therapies. When I give her a bath, I thank God for keeping her safe despite the times she had seizures in the tub.

Lord, your Word says the joy of the Lord is my strength. I need Your kind of strength and I desperately want your kind of joy! Help me to dwell on positive things and recognize the many things for which I can be genuinely thankful. Let me find delight in Your holy Words of Scripture and Your Word living in me through the Holy Spirit. Show me how to be humble, courageous, and gracious in all of my relationships, but particularly the difficult ones. Thank you for the promise to use my obedience in shaping my attitudes and filling my heart with true joy. AMEN

Chapter 12:
SHARING — *Is it worth it?*

One day Jesus encountered a man who had been blind from birth. John's Gospel tells us that the disciples asked, *"Rabbi, who sinned, this man or his parents, that he was born blind?"* Jesus' answer is a promising one for those of us waiting to see God's glory revealed in our difficult circumstances.

> *"Neither this man nor his parents sinned,"* said Jesus, *"but this happened so that the work of God might be displayed in his life. As long as it is day, we must do the work of Him who sent Me."*
> JOHN 9:3-4

Jesus' answer demonstrates that we all have both opportunity and responsibility in displaying Glory. And we cannot be a display of anything if our lives and hearts are not visible, even engaged with others.

When Carly was born and for several years after that, we attended a church that supported us endlessly. They became for us part of the visible expression of love from an otherwise invisible God. What we had been so afraid to ask for, God had abundantly provided. That Body of believers stood by our family in prayer, hope, and a myriad of practical helps. For years and even now, they continue to be among our most enthusiastic encouragers and prayer warriors. They taught us about what it really means to share in ministry.

It is no coincidence to us that the name of that church is Vision of Glory.

These have been difficult years. And there will be more. But there are ripples of God's greatness picking up exciting speed. Our family loves to reminisce about the countless relational intersections that hold such deep meaning for us. Sometimes those connections have been for our benefit and other times for the benefit of someone else. God has given us a picture of the ripples of glory He is painting around Carly. And as people's lives, including our own, are being transformed, it's a real thrill to stop from time to time, take notice, celebrate, and share together our gratitude to God. As you look at more commemorating "rocks" with us — from our journey and from the Scriptures — may you be inspired by the Holy Spirit to share the Lord's handiwork in your own story.

Life's Intersections Cause Magnificent Ripples

When my mom went to the mailbox that day in 1999 and found a flyer asking for help with Judd's program, an enormous ripple effect was gaining strength and the lives of hundreds of people were changed forever. We lost touch with Judd over the years, which is sad. Imagine the joys we could share if he and his family knew about the magnificent ripple effect of healing that he inspired! Life is like that though. We rarely have any idea how significant the seemingly insignificant things we do end up being.

We know God starts working His glory through us from the moment we are born. However, it was about the time that Carly started her home-based neurodevelopmental therapy program that the ripples of God's power on her life started becoming obvious to us.

When over sixty volunteers were streaming in and out of our home on a weekly basis, we could see God using that community for our collective nourishment. There are numerous stories we could tell about all we learned from each other, how we encouraged each other, and how we saw Jesus together.

We love to tell people about Lois. We actually had several beautiful Loises with us in the early years. We had a lot of fun with that fact. This particular Lois had suffered from a stroke within the year before coming to help Carly. She had experienced a good degree of recovery but her healing process seemed to have plateaued. She was concerned about her ability to contribute due to a very weak, almost immobile arm, and some instability on her feet. But she really wanted to help. Needing timekeepers and list checkers, we encouraged her to come and try on those roles. This was a woman with great courage and enthusiasm though and so it wasn't long before she was trying to help us with the cross-patterning activity too. It is a rather rigorous exercise to perform, especially if the recipient is resistant. Carly was usually cooperative but she did gain strength and coordination quickly enough to be quite a handful once in a while.

Before too long, Lois started arriving on her shifts with news about increased strength she was experiencing. Her help with Carly was proving therapeutic for her as well. Lois began studying many of the things we were doing and wondering about what it must feel like for this little girl to do them and how it might be impacting her. Lois also began to wonder if any of those activities would aid in her own healing. She started coming to shifts telling about different things she'd tried to do and what it felt like to do them. We would all get very excited. She began to notice subtle but important changes in what she was feeling, how she was gaining strength and stability, and how former function was returning.

Sometimes there were exercises Lois wished she could do along with Carly but something got in the way. For example, due to knee problems, Lois couldn't get on her knees to do the weight-bearing activity on her palms in the way that Carly did. Yet she was convinced it could be helpful to her. We brainstormed ideas with Lois about how she could adapt Carly's exercises and Lois came up with some ideas of her own. After awhile, she was taking initiative, on faith, and trying to do Carly's exercises at home believing they would be helpful in her own recovery.

Lois became a voice for Carly, helping us understand the value of what we were doing with her on a whole new level. Since

Carly couldn't tell us what she was feeling, there were often clues we would get from Lois' experience that helped us understand and improve on ways we were going about Carly's activities.

And then one day, Lois sat down on our couch with checklist and timer in hand. And with a big grin on her face, she began her story. "I'm knitting again!" she shared. "I haven't been able to knit for almost two years because I couldn't pinch my fingers on this hand together and I couldn't feel the yarn. Last weekend, I realized I could start making yarn balls because the feeling in my fingers was returning. And yesterday I started a knitting project." She had been doing one of Carly's tactile input activities for just two weeks while watching TV.

The joy of the Lord was our strength that day. And we saw the ripples.

From Carly's earliest days, the nursery coordinator at our church deeply empathized with our "colicky" baby. Every Sunday when Carly screamed, Marcia recounted stories about the extremely difficult days she had endured when her oldest child, Amanda, was a baby. At first, we were offended when people like this mom seemed to misunderstand the severity of Carly's inconsolableness. We really didn't think anyone could relate to what we were going through. However, we got to know each other much better when Marcia offered to become one of our first volunteers.

With each shift Marcia worked, we learned more about the years of challenge Amanda and her family had been experiencing. Marcia humbly and tearfully admitted that Amanda's poor ability to handle changes in routine and even mildly stressful situations were actually somewhat destructive to their whole family system. Marcia grieved that her fifteen-year-old daughter was now unlikely to get a driver's license. She was certain that college would not be in her future as she increasingly struggled with schoolwork and would not likely be able to cope with various aspects of being away from home.

To Marcia's credit, she learned all she could about sensory processing disorders and quickly became an advocate for Amanda with dramatic results. Despite many obstacles with insurance and healthcare providers, Amanda was assessed for sensory processing concerns. It was determined that she did, in fact, have some sensory disorganization and occupational therapy was promptly initiated both at home and in a clinic.

Within weeks, Marcia was reporting encouraging progress. About a year later, Amanda changed schools and soon after got her driver's license. Home life for Marcia's family was peaceful in a way that it had not been for many years. Then one day, we all sat in church filled with joy as this once socially awkward young woman delivered her confirmation testimony with poise and confidence. At the end, Amanda read a self-composed poem. And the congregation wept. Three years later, Amanda went to college.

And there were ripples.

Remember, Judd had inspired Carly. Well, next, Carly had the opportunity to inspire Nathan. Nathan's program started, with God's Divine timing, right at the point when Carly's development required more one-on-one support so we no longer needed teams of three all day long. Funding had also become available for us to hire a paid staff person. That meant releasing our volunteers, many of whom were disappointed at not being needed anymore. So they enthusiastically embraced the opportunity to drive a new direction in town and they headed for Nathan's house.

Talk about ripples, look at what his mom wrote in a "Nathan Update" two years later:

NATHAN UPDATE Week# 104

What a time we've had watching God work in our family - showing His power and His provision.

On August 1, 2001 (almost three years old), Nathan could crawl on his belly, smile, roll over, be cute, sit if he was propped up with pillows, play on the computer, drink from a cup held by someone else, laugh, eat most food if it was cut into small pieces, be outside in an infant swing, sit in a high chair with support, ride in a grocery cart with the strap fastened and side support, watch others play games, use his left hand but not his right hand, touch our hearts with love beyond description.

After one year of program which included 11,000 masks - 300 hours of cross patterning - 2,500 volunteer man hours - 800 reading words - countless prayers...

On August 1, 2002, Nathan could get into a sitting position with no assistance, smile, creep up on his hands and knees, kneel up to a table to play, use the computer better than most forty year olds, drink from a handle cup with no assistance, drink from a straw, bite larger pieces of food and safely chew/swallow, be cute, support his weight for over five minutes while holding onto an overhead bar, creep up the stairs with minimal assistance, creep down the stairs with no assistance, laugh, read at a first grade level, sit in the sand box and play for hours on end, sit in a booster chair, sit on a stool and move his feet to turn his body 180 degrees, play age appropriate board games, enjoy make-believe play, use a pincer grasp with his left hand, use his right hand functionally, do many tasks bi-manually, turn circles in the creeping position, crawl over objects up to eight inches high, use his body and hands to balance, walk under an overhead bar with help for his hands and feet, and touch our hearts with love beyond description.

After a second year of program which included another 11,000 masks - 300 hours of assisted walking - 700 volunteer man hours - 130 hours of gravity free - lots of hopping, standing and cruising around tables...

On August 1, 2003, Nathan could walk 120 meters in thirty minutes only needing help to grip the overhead bar with his right hand, giggle infectiously, use a low table to pull himself from a kneeling to a standing position, hop three feet off the floor in his "harness," cruise fifteen meters around a chest high table in just ten minutes (moving his legs and hands on his own, but needing some support to bear his full weight), stand in his stander for ninety minutes per day (only needing straps at his hips, chest and right thigh), stand with no support for five seconds, win the long eyelash contest when judged by the people behind us in the checkout line, say "thank you" and "mama" in a way most people can understand, use a "hand over hand" technique (yup, his left AND right hand) to pull a balloon down from the ceiling, get in and out of a side-sitting position with no assistance, use sign language in such a creative way even total strangers can figure out what he is saying, dance while holding only his partner's hands for support, and touch our hearts with love beyond description.

We give God the honor and glory for each improvement Nathan has realized. We also give thanks to you - your prayers, love, friendship, discernment, ideas, and kindness were daily encouragements to us! We know the Lord will complete this good work He has begun and we look forward to the mighty miracles He will accomplish in the next twelve months.

In The Power of His Love,

Barb

Since those days, Carly has inspired Victoria, Sophie, and Courtney as well as numerous other challenged children. In turn, those children are inspiring others to find their potential through ground breaking educational methods. In some cases, we are sure, lives have even be saved.

More ripples.

Over the past six years, more than twenty people have been part of our support staff helping us care for Carly. Most, though not all, of these women started working with Carly during high school or immediately following. The older staff usually came with a history within the medical field or some nature of experience helping children with special needs. All of them developed an increased passion for nurturing the developmental, health, and spiritual potential of others while working with Carly.

For many of those who started working with Carly before their education was complete, time with Carly significantly impacted the direction of their post-graduate education and careers. On that list of Carly's "retired caregivers" there is already a nutrition professional and a teacher of special education students. We are also told there will be a doctor, possibly a pharmacist, a physical therapist, an occupational therapist, and more special education teachers. Just imagine the number of lives that will be touched by these women. Most exciting of all is that all of these women love the Lord Jesus Christ and will bring to their careers and their own children the fragrance and knowledge of Christ that draws people into deeper and life-changing relationships with God.

Yet again, more ripples for the Kingdom.

Very young children are learning from the modeling and encouragement of their parents that, even at their age, they can be powerful ministers of blessing and vehicles for God's power. One spring day, eight of our friends' children from three different families came to our house and spent almost two hours helping me (Lisa) make customized therapy videos for Carly. They enthusiastically modeled activities like counting, self-help skills, and word usage, all of which were targeted to very specific things we were working on with Carly.

Watching them work cooperatively to help us in the battle for her progress reminded me of the very cool thing God did a long time ago with Moses when the Israelites were under attack by the Amalekites. Exodus chapter 17 tells how Moses sent his very good friend Joshua, a great warrior, to fight the Amalekites. During the battle, Moses stood on top of the hill with the staff of God in his hands. As long as Moses held his hands with the staff high up in the air, the Israelites were winning. But whenever Moses lowered his hands, the Amalekites were winning. The battle was long and Moses would get tired. He couldn't keep holding his arms up. So Moses took his brother Aaron and his friend Hur with him to the top of that hill. Whenever he was too tired to keep holding up his arms, Aaron and Hur stood beside him and held up each of his arms. With the help of these mighty men Moses and the Israelites won the battle. God gave these men a very special friendship and showed them how to work together for God's glory.

Sometimes Carly made progress and we felt like she was winning her battles. Other times, she would get tired and we got tired and it didn't feel like any of us were winning. But God used those kids and their friendship with Carly to strengthen her. They helped her get excited about learning and showed her how to do things that she had to work hard to understand. They still do this every time they play with her. It's like they are holding her up to Jesus because she can't fight by herself.

Many friends have helped us in that sort of way, including other children. The day of that "movie shoot," as they proudly called it, our family was very tired and very discouraged. We felt like God sent them to hold us up and help us with a very important job we couldn't do by ourselves. Our friends and their children are learning so much with us about how amazingly God works. And those children are going to carry these lessons with them into lives that will be incredibly powerful for the Kingdom!

The ripples are extending beyond the horizons now.

The "Carly Updates" gave us an early sense that we were actually able to do ministry for God's Kingdom out of our experiences with Carly. Those updates started out simply as a tool to communicate consistently and efficiently with out-of-town family as well as volunteers who wanted to share in celebrating Carly's progress and praying for our needs.

In January of 2007, a number of people came around us once more when Lisa had to have a hysterectomy. After petitioning our "Carly Update" community for crisis help and seeing them come through for us yet again, Lisa wrote:

> 1 John 4:12 says, *"No one has seen God. But if we love one another, God lives in us, and His love has been brought to full expression through us."* We sure feel like we've experienced God through many of you, especially again in the last couple of weeks! We have sat down to several tasty meals prepared by friends. People have been coming and going in the mornings to help me care for Carly and get her off to school after lunch. Several of you even lingered to sort or fold some laundry along the way. Steve, Marifran, and Shelley helped with transportation duties for piano lessons, safety patrols, and choir. I have received

beautiful cards and several bouquets of flowers, taken phone calls from caring people just wanting to check in, and treasured every email. A couple of you just came to sit and visit (a real treat when all you can do is lie around for days on end). I'm really grateful for those comforting and strengthening words people have shared from Scripture to keep my mind and heart fixed on Jesus. And we feel literally **carried** through the ups and the downs of life when we know you are praying. The cumulative effect of so many people reaching out in a variety of ways is profound. People are so busy. I think for that reason most of all, it's very hard to ask each other for help. Most of us will only ask for help when we're desperate and then the other times we just try to press through. I believe more than ever that we miss out on so much of God's fullness when we live like that. I can really say, "His love has been brought to full expression through you." I challenge you today to consider how God may be prompting you to **ask** for help or **give** sacrificially of your time. By the way, it's always easier to give than to ask but not necessarily better or more righteous. Do the uncomfortable and risky thing. Let a few people know you need their prayers. Locate a promise in Scripture to email a friend. Please know that whatever you have done to help us out, we have received it with a great sense of blessing. No matter how insignificant your giving feels, it is powerful to us.

The reality is that we wouldn't even be writing this book if it weren't for the support of a community of people who continue to step into the river with us. Everyone leads extremely busy lives yet many have taken time to help us and encourage us and pray for us. It's not even the large chunks of time that people have given that are the biggest deal (although those are amazing). It has been the cumulative sum of many people giving even a little that has made it possible for us be the parents we are, do the work we do, and have the relationship we have.

The daily reality of parenting Carly should never have allowed us time to write a book. The logistics alone would have been insurmountable. Yet affirming emails gave us confidence and the prayers of our closest family and friends reassured us that we had something of value to share. By their giving to us in the Lord's name, they have enabled us to give something back to you. What amazing economy! What beauty!

We never expected the "Carly Updates" to become the source of inspiration and encouragement that they were. While keeping us accountable to acknowledging things worthy of praise to God, the updates allowed us to receive prayer, empathy, and affirmation from others. We never expected it would become part of a ministry of sorts. Feedback from both friends and strangers have proven time and again that God's power to use us transcends our ability to understand how he does so!

Someone we have never met read a "Carly Update" that had been forwarded to her. She responded by saying:

"Thank you for uplifting our spirits and listening to that calm still voice inside that we need to hear. When examples like you come along, it soothes the spirits of people who are in such torment…God gives them that strength through you. God is using you in awesome ways whether you know it or not. Don't ever stop…you have definitely been given the gift of making the day because of your obedience to tell the truth."

Are you seeing ripples in your story? Have you been afraid to share them? We understand that a number of things can still the voice inside that wants to tell the world about what God is doing. We feel awkward even copying down that woman's email because it could be perceived as self-congratulatory. Even if our motive is delight in seeing God's handiwork lifted up, Satan lures us into logic that suggests we should never boast. The Apostle Paul repeats the words of the prophet Jeremiah when he says, *"Let him who boasts, boast in the Lord."* (1 Corinthians 1:31)

Don't ever let the enemy silence you about what God is doing. Maybe your motives aren't perfectly pure. Pray for increased integrity and godliness and then shout God's praises to the mountaintops! Nothing can bring God glory if it isn't seen!

Maybe you think your situation is different from ours. Do you think God's fingerprints are more obvious in our life scenario? Well, that's a lie. If you aren't seeing evidence of God's fruitfulness flowing in and around you, then consider why. There might be sin keeping you turned away from God so you can't see what He's doing. You may have self-esteem issues and need to learn more about your identity in Christ. But for most of us, it's just a matter of having a weak radar.

During a mission trip to Belize, Central America, I (Lisa) heard someone marveling at how God's presence seemed so tangible there. "God is visible all over the place here! Barely an hour goes by when we haven't seen Him answer one of our prayers," she said.

My response was quick, maybe too quick to seem humble but it came out of years learning the truth. "God is just as present at home in America. We're just too busy to notice."

We can learn to live every day with the kind of prayerful focus and attentiveness to the Holy Spirit that we have when we are on a special mission half way across the world. But it might mean we need to slow down and re-prioritize from time to time. In any case, we need to keep our antennae up — stay on the lookout for ripples. We can ask God to strengthen our radar to see Him at work around us. The heavens are not the only display of God's glory on this side of eternity!

What does it mean for you to put God's glory on display? Does it mean sharing a testimony with your friends? Does it mean mentioning something about God's blessings to you in a conversation with someone in your family? Does it mean writing a journal, making a scrapbook, designing a website, painting a picture, singing a song? Does it mean running a marathon, making a meal for a busy friend, coaching your child's sports team? Does it mean having lunch with a fellow student or hurting co-worker to listen with a heart like Jesus'?

We Must Take Each Other to Jesus

Sometimes people ask, "What can we do to help?" And sometimes an idea comes to mind that makes sense and fits for that person. But often, we cannot give an answer simply because we are too overwhelmed or too much on autopilot to think. It is even more difficult when people simply say, "let me know if there's anything we can do." Particularly in an overwhelming season, we don't have energy to give it consideration later and may even be inclined to believe nothing can be delegated.

The fact is, some of our responsibilities can be shared but we tend to cling even more tightly to our usual routines and comfort zones when life feels so out of control. At least initially, even the simplest change in the routine can feel like one more thing to keep track of. Will we remember that someone offered to drive the girls to piano lessons next Wednesday? Sometimes we have to remind ourselves that the temporary relief from a simple responsibility would help move us in the direction of getting our mental, emotional, and spiritual house in order. When all is said and done, we are especially blessed by people who make specific offers of help like, "Would it be okay for me to bring you a meal next Tuesday?" or "Could I come and mow your lawn this weekend?" or "Could I help with Carly during Sunday School so that the two of you could worship at church together?" or simply "How can I be praying for you?"

In the second chapter of Mark's Gospel, we read about a paralyzed man who had incredible friends. They not only helped to meet his practical needs, but they facilitated his spiritual healing as well.

Jesus was in Capernaum and many people had gathered to see him. It was like a big reunion. Jesus was preaching the Word and there was such a large crowd, that there wasn't even room outside the door for all of the people to get close to him. A paralyzed man, brought by his friends, came in faith that God might heal him. His friends were so loyal and so enthusiastic about Jesus' now well-known capabilities for healing, that they started thinking very creatively about how to make sure their friend got his face-to-face with the Lord.

We don't know if the man's friends had the idea of taking him to Jesus. Did the man's friends insist on taking Him? Or was the man so overwhelmed by his paralysis that he was desperate to see if Jesus' reputation for healing would extend to him? I love to imagine that he had the kind of friends who said, "Hey man, we've gotta take you to see this guy. We know you're tired. Don't worry about a thing. We'll coordinate it. The rest of the guys will be over in a few minutes and we'll take you. It's no problem. We're just glad that there is something we can do that might be helpful and we're excited to be part of the possibilities with you!"

And then when they got there, the masses of people were overwhelming. Do you think they knew ahead of time that the size of the crowds would demand that they dig through a roof to get their friend to Jesus? Did they use their bare hands to carve away at the clay and straw, or had they anticipated the need to bring shovels or knives along with some type of pulley system to lower their friend down?

In any case, their faith impressed Jesus so He forgave the man's sins **and** made him well. This caused quite a stir among the teachers of the law who considered such claims about forgiveness to be blasphemy. But what an amazing, probably unexpected result it was for the man and four of his friends to realize that not only could he walk away in full view of the crowds but he did so as a spiritually free man!

We all need friends like that! These guys have really set a standard for us now. Oh, to have friends who are so creative, so enthusiastic, so committed to us that they would do everything they possibly could for us. The best kind of friends are not only those who are willing to carry our mat and meet our practical needs, but they are the ones who will crash through all obstacles to help us come to the feet of Jesus.

Our community of support is not typical. We have received an unusual degree of practical and spiritual help from our extended family, friends, church, and even strangers. This is amazing and humbling to us. Our hearts ache to think that others are enduring such struggles without it. There have been periods of time when we felt ignored, abandoned and invisible. But in the grand scheme of things, the number of mat-bearers we have in our lives is remarkable.

The support we have received sometimes seems endless:

- folding our laundry,
- mowing our lawn,
- shoveling our snow,
- hanging our Christmas lights,
- making us meals (we even had a neighbor who cooked a meal for us every Monday night — for a year!),
- attending a prayer gathering, initiated by a friend, specifically for the purpose of praying for our family in a season of despair,
- coordinating food co-ops (to make available and economical the nutritional lifestyle we needed),
- giving us places to stay on vacations,
- providing us with a place away from home for writing retreats,
- helping with Carly's many therapies,
- providing respite care,
- building equipment for Carly from the adjustable inclined slide, to the carpet board, to the patterning table, to the brachiated ladder, to the slant board, to Grandpa's "superdeeduper anti-tip chair,"
- performing in and producing custom videos and audiotapes for Carly's therapy,
- loaning us used toys and videos,
- creating a CD of specially-selected songs in hopes that they would help Carly relax at night,
- offering ideas about how to help Carly sleep, eat independently and manage seizures,
- helping with painting, wallpapering, landscaping and other household projects,
- sewing Carly's adapted pajamas and bibs,
- knitting us a prayer shawl,
- driving kids to lessons and practices,

- offering to help Carly in a bowling league,
- gathering a group of women for an afternoon to make and freeze gallons of Carly's special broth,
- encouraging us with a song dedicated to Larry and Carly at a concert,
- having a stranger in a restaurant give us a pastry, an encouraging word, and a note with Scripture and a prayer written on it,
- giving us tickets to a Bible conference,
- sending many many emails in response to "Carly Updates,"
- and praying like warriors!

We have also been on the receiving end of one of the most creative acts of merciful service that we have ever seen. Larry's aunt and uncle live across the country — too far away, it could have seemed, to make a meaningful contribution to our practical needs for help. But that has never stopped Aunt Sylvia who has had everyone in their circles praying for us. A crafty woman in mind and talent, she pulled together some crafty friends and they stitched beautiful cross-shaped bookmarks as a gratitude gift to each of our volunteers back in the year 2000. They stitched sixty of them! And then, a year later, they crocheted crock-pot knob potholders. Another sixty of them! Year after year, she would check in with me. "How many people do you have helping now?" She would mysteriously suggest that something would be coming in the mail soon. And sure enough, there were potato bakers one year, microwave hot pads another.

The ways people have reached out to help us is nothing short of indescribable. Overwhelming mercy. Overwhelming grace. Now tell us that doesn't look like the glory of God to you!

In the situation with the paralytic, those friends did so much. They risked embarrassment and the anger of the poor guy whose roof they had just wrecked. For all of the practical ways people have helped us, the times when we have been personally escorted to the feet of Jesus are especially profound. Friends have sent us Scripture verses by email, prayed with us over the phone, walked throughout the house claiming it for Jesus so the enemy could have no foothold in Carly's sleeplessness, sat together in a living room for Bible Study and prayer, challenged us to see Jesus in our situation differently, confronted us when they saw habitual sin in our life, and held us accountable to being in prayer and reading God's Word.

When our closest friends sense our discouragement, they often pray immediately with us. Even on the phone. Not even "I'll be praying for you" is good enough for them. They take time to do it right now, even if right now is inconvenient. Now that's really "going to the mat" for a friend.

One example of a note from a friend demonstrates the kind of encouragement we have received many times via email:

> "I am praying for you continually. I can only imagine your daily efforts to make life for Carly, Erin, Alex, and yourselves one of comfort and ease. You all amaze me... even in the hard times it shows and reflects God's glory. I will pray specifically that God's strength will be yours in this week to come. I will pray that God will move you the next step, and then the next, and then the next. Psalm 16 comes to mind as it has been one of great hope and strength for me."

How can a person not melt into the love of Jesus when touched by the soothing balms of words and friendships like that!

All throughout the New Testament people wanted to be near Jesus because great and marvelous things happened there. How easily we can miss the obvious—our goal needs to be to get near to God and we must surround ourselves with people who will help us accomplish that. For that is where we need to be so that we can participate — like the paralytic did — in the display of His glory!

When the Work is God's, It is Transformational

Lots of people do good things. After all, humankind was made in the image of God. So there is bound to be something of His goodness reflected in everyone. But of course, not all lives are yielded to the One True God. Not all good things are done for His benefit.

Ministry done in the name of Jesus, for the purpose of bringing glory to God, has a unique capacity. The life of a Christ follower who has experienced comfort from God through the Holy Spirit has the opportunity and indwelling power to do more than just help someone feel encouraged—it has the power to bring others into life.

> *Praise be to the God and Father of our Lord Jesus Christ, the Father of compassion and the God of all comfort, who comforts us in all our troubles, so that we can comfort those in any trouble with the comfort we ourselves have received from God. For just as the sufferings of Christ flow over into our lives, so also through Christ our comfort overflows. Indeed, in our hearts we felt the sentence of death. But this happened that we might not rely on ourselves but on God, who raises the dead...and he will deliver us.*
> 2 CORINTHIANS 1:3-5 AND 9-10

Carly is ten years old now and her life has been powerfully affected by countless people who passionately love Jesus and have faithfully prayed with us for her. She continues to make developmental progress and amaze us with her potential. She has been seizure free for over three years. In recent months, she has had many nights of ten or more consecutive hours of sleep. She walks well by herself and has a belly laugh that rivals the song of angels. Her frequent snuggles and cuddly nature are nothing short of extraordinary!

Perhaps most remarkably, Carly has a vocabulary of word approximations that is rare and unexpected of someone with Angelman Syndrome, especially someone with the "deletion positive" scenario. Among the forty words she approximates, Carly gives spontaneous hugs and articulates a clear, "I love you." We are celebrating that her quality of life and ours is quite possibly as gorgeous as it will get on this side of heaven.

Carly's life has been transformed and, as a result, so has ours. We look at each other often and ask, "Who really needed the healing anyway?" Our story, like everyone's this here on earth, isn't finished yet. Life is a journey. Carly's healing is a process after all—as is ours. God's glory is all around us, all through us, and all consuming when we take time to look.

Like intersecting ripples on the water, God uses the intersections of our lives (the thorny parts most of all) to create a beautiful picture for all the world to see. It is the picture of His power and love at work within and among us. If you ask us, "Do you think you can see God?" we could say, "We can hardly see anything else!"

Many times since that day in the hospital so many years ago, we groaned that desperate cry, "It wasn't supposed to be this way!" Yet over and over again we have learned that God squeezes life's richest and fullest blessings out of every trial. The blessings God brings out of challenge and suffering are always more profound than we imagined they could be when we press into a loving relationship with Him. We increasingly experience tangible expressions of His deeply loving presence among us through the intersections of our lives with others. Maybe, yes quite probably, this is exactly the way it was supposed to be.

Jesus knew all along what suffering lay ahead for Him, but He lived every moment for His mission — His ministry was to see God's good come out of every problem, every sin, every need, every relational intersection. That is no different than how we are called to live. Just imagine for a moment how God's power would be magnified all around us if you and I really lived that out!

The seventeenth chapter of the Gospel of John recounts Jesus' prayer at the Garden of Gethsemane. It is a somewhat lengthy prayer, but well worth re-reading. In those intimate moments between Father and Son, Jesus mentions glory nine times! This was a focused man.

There was much Jesus had to say to His Father about the mission He was about to see fulfilled. In John 17:1-4, he begins his prayer saying:

"Father, the time has come. Glorify your Son, that your Son may glorify You. ...Now this is eternal life: that they may know you, the only true God, and Jesus Christ, whom you have sent. I have brought you glory on earth by completing the work you

gave me to do. And now, Father, glorify me in your presence
with the glory I had with you before the world began."

But lest we think that the flow of God's glory is reserved exclusively within Himself, consider how Jesus went on to pray for his friends and disciples. Jesus says, "

And glory has come to me through them."
JOHN 17:10

Those relationships were a precious blessing to Jesus. Christ followers have the capacity to bring glory unto God. Future believers were to have that same capacity. Did you notice in that prayer that Jesus also prayed for you? He prayed for all believers to come in the future. He said, *"I pray also for those who will believe in me through* (the disciples') *message, that all of them may be one, Father, just as you are in me and I am in you."* The purpose for that kind of unity with us, according to Jesus, was *"to let the world know that you sent me and have loved them even as you have loved me"* (John 17:23). Jesus said,

"I have given them the glory that you gave me, that they may be one as we are one"
JOHN 17:22

We really do share in that potential — in that privilege. We can be an instrument of God's glory. We can join that glory-filled adventure towards eternal presence with our Creator who started loving us even before any of our days came to be (Psalm 139:16).

Jesus' excitement about sharing life now and forever with us was expressed in those Gethsemane moments.

"Father, I want those you have given me to be with me where I am, and to see my glory, the glory you have given me because you loved me before the creation of the world."
JOHN 17:24

Within minutes or just a few hours of this prayer, Jesus' journey to the cross was launched once and for all with Judas' kiss. Did that nullify all of Jesus' dreams? It would have if Jesus' death had been the end of the story. But it wasn't.

The resurrected Jesus appeared to the grieving Mary Magdalene with this reassurance:

> *"I am returning to my Father and your Father, to my God and your God."*
> JOHN 20:17

Later that same day, Jesus appeared in the flesh to his disciples. An incredible thing happened:

> *And with that, he breathed on them and said, "Receive the Holy Spirit."*
> JOHN 20:22

Jesus was very much alive. No amount of suffering, torture, ridicule, denial or life-taking crucifixion could keep Him down. Despite His dying, Jesus was quite literally living and breathing. Because of that power, that victory, that hope, it is not necessary for any amount of suffering to keep you down either. You share Christ's story from humble beginning, through the agonizing middle, and all the way to the glorious end!

> *"For you did not receive a spirit that makes you a slave again to fear, but you received the Spirit of sonship. And by Him we cry, 'Abba, Father.' The Spirit himself testifies with our spirit that we are God's children. Now if we are children, then we are heirs — heirs of God and co-heirs with Christ, if indeed we share in his sufferings in order that we may also share in his glory."*
> ROMANS 8:15-17

WHEN YOU PRACTICE SHARING...

ENJOY THE RIPPLES
OF GOD'S ALL-CONSUMING COMFORT

Praise be to the God and Father of our Lord Jesus Christ, the Father of compassion and the God of all comfort, who comforts us in all our troubles, so that we can comfort those in any trouble with the comfort we ourselves have received from God. For just as the sufferings of Christ flow over into our lives, so also through Christ our comfort overflows.
2 CORINTHIANS 1:3-5

Consider these things while praying for God to increase your vision of His glory:
• Who helps carry your mat (bears your burdens)?
• Who are the people in your life willing to do whatever it takes to make sure you stay at the feet of Jesus? (If there are no roof-crashers in your circle of close friends, consider expanding or pruning it.)
• How have the ripples from other people's lives impacted your life in positive ways for God's kingdom?
• What kinds of things may God be prompting you to do so that His glory in you is shared with others and magnified by Him?

Lord, my situation is not hopeless to you. Help me learn to ask for and graciously receive help from others as a blessing from You in my life. Help me to understand the value of my vulnerability. Teach me how to share the adverse circumstances of my life authentically and transparently. Show me how to be a mat-bearer for people around me too; help me to draw people towards you. I really need more enthusiastic mat-bearers in my life—people who will keep me coming near to You. Please surround me with people who will creatively and specifically offer support and show me how to let the willing help! Show me how to receive humbly and graciously. Let me not be any obstacle to the release of Your power in my life for the glory of Your name! AMEN

Epilogue

We never imagined, as we sat in the wake of our "island run" so many years ago, that we would still be running this race of life after years without satisfying physical rest. We never imagined that we would find ourselves asking life's toughest questions about faith and hope and joy and God's purposes under such overwhelming circumstances. Did we ever imagine that something of the thorny sides of our life could look anything like this? A book? A tear-stained love offering to the Lord?

Well, truth be told, the thought had actually crossed our minds. We were professional writers after all. And with all of those "Carly Updates," we had been told a time or two "you should write a book!" Still, to get to this season of our journey is incredible to us. It's nothing short of miraculous that the Lord even carved out enough moments for our publishing project to happen at all. Even when our official "book project" seemed to be making painstakingly slow progress — endlessly interrupted by life — we never imagined that the first full draft would be written within a twelve month span and completed just two days before Christmas. How God did this at all, let alone in the midst of the busy holiday season, was an amazing gift. Perhaps if there was another chapter, it would symbolically be called "Our Season of Christmas!" It is so humbling and exciting to see God at work in our midst!

God uses all kinds of talents, stories, and relationships to magnify His goodness. There will always be a more entertaining or heartbreaking story than ours. Perhaps even yours. But each one of our stories has special potential, when surrendered to the power of the Holy Spirit, to resonate with certain people during certain seasons. God knows the times and places where your transparency and compassion will plant seeds and reap harvests for His kingdom. Imagine letting people see God through you during a phone call, over a cup of coffee, walking one of the fairways of a golf course, standing in line at the grocery store, sharing a prayer request, writing an email, shoveling snow in your neighbor's driveway, or sitting on a school bus. What glory there is in making your skills, experiences, and compassion available to Him! What glory there is in receiving and sharing the Holy Spirit's comfort!

Your story matters, regardless of what kind of season you are in. It matters to God. And it matters to other people. The transforming power of the Holy Spirit can use you to minister to people you know and people you don't yet know. Have you been hearing his promptings? He is calling you to come sit with Him, to be still and listen. Are you embracing the comfort He offers? Do you hear Him telling you to reach out a little more? Is he challenging you to try something new, even taking just one step at a time?

Are you going to step into the river?
Go ahead.
Take the plunge!
God's ripples in here are absolutely stunning!

Humble yourselves, therefore, under God's mighty hand, that he may lift you up in due time. Cast all your anxiety on him because he cares for you. Be self-controlled and alert. Your enemy the devil prowls around like a roaring lion looking for someone to devour. Resist him, standing firm in the faith, because you know that your brothers throughout the world are undergoing the same kind of sufferings.
And the God of all grace, who called you to his eternal glory in Christ, after you have suffered a little while, will himself restore you and make you strong, firm and steadfast.
To him be the power for ever and ever.
1 Peter 5:6-11

Amen.

Carly at three days old.

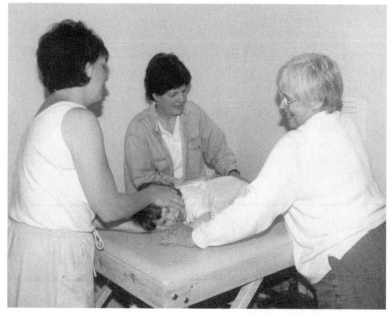

Inputting the cross-pattern was critical.

Our first family photos rarely captured a calm Carly.

Learning to crawl with her "wings."

The famous Kindergarten hallway walk.

No fear and a love for speed!

This is the day Carly graduated from trike to bike
with help from her sisters, Alex and Erin.

Experiencing the joy of cuddling!

Carly is thrilled to be moving!

HOST YOUR OWN
Book Party!

In your Home
or at your Church

Read, Meet & Share
Book Party!

You're invited to an adventure in fellowship and life-changing inspiration. Here's how it works. Before the party, each of us will read the book *Finding Glory in the Thorns*. Then we'll get together to meet the authors, Larry and Lisa Jamieson. They will answer questions and we'll all share how God is inspiring us.

WHEN?
Your Time & Date Here

WHERE?
Your Party Location
& Address Here

PARTY HOST
Your Name or Group Here

Paperback, 204 pages. $12.99
Order at **www.findingglory.com**

Join us for food and great fellowship. Share inspiring stories, meet the authors, get your books autographed!
Please RSVP to Your Name at ###-###-#### or youremail@youremail.

Gather your Group...
Friends, Neighbors, Book Club or Church Group

- Meet the authors and have your books signed
- Share good food, friendly conversation, and inspiring stories

For more information go to www.findingglory.com